LESS STRESS, PLEASE

Though this book is designed for group study, it is also intended for your personal enjoyment and spiritual growth. A leader's guide is available from your local bookstore or from your publisher.

Beacon Hill Press of Kansas City
Kansas City, Missouri

Editor
Stephen M. Miller

Editorial Assistant
Rebecca Privett

Editorial Committee
Randy Cloud
Thomas Mayse
Stephen M. Miller
Carl Pierce
Gene Van Note

Cover design by Royce Ratcliff
Cover photo by Comstock

Copyright 1992
Printed in the United States of America
ISBN: 083-411-4070

Bible Credits

10   9   8

Contents

1

Stress:
You Can't Avoid It,
but You Can Control It

Even if It Involves
a One-Ton Bull Moose

by Vicki Hesterman

IT PROMISED to be a relaxing trip. I had just graduated from college and was off with one of my best friends on our first wilderness trek in the mountains. Both our boyfriends had been wary about two young women camping alone, but we wanted one last adventure before going our separate ways. What better place to relax and reminisce than in the shadows of Wyoming's gorgeous Grand Tetons? Sounds like a guaranteed stress reducer, right?

But as Nancy and I relaxed around the campfire and watched the rosy colors of the mountain sunset fade through the trees, a cow moose and her calf came wandering toward us through the underbrush. We tensed up and waited, motionless, for several moments, until the animals noticed us and abruptly turned back into the forest.

With that excitement behind us, we doused our fire, crawled into the relative safety of our tiny orange tent, and

squirmed into our sleeping bags. Before we could get comfortable, we heard a crashing in the woods. A huge bull
moose was coming through the shadows, heading straight
for us. We had apparently pitched our tent on his favorite
spot, on soft pine needles near the lake.

My heart was pounding. My throat was dry. My hands
were sweating.

I had all the symptoms of what psychology experts say
is the normal "fight or flight" reaction to extreme stress. But
I couldn't use the defenses my body was preparing. Fighting a ton of wild mammal with my bare hands wasn't an
option.

Neither was fleeing. The little I knew about animals
called moose was they were nearsighted, quick-tempered,
fast on their feet, and inclined to charge anything that
threatened them. By the time I could manage to get out of
the sleeping bag and tent and to my feet, any healthy
moose not on medication could have made short work of
me.

It seemed best to stay in the tent and be still. "Don't
move or make a sound," I whispered as quietly as I could.

The night was long and sleepless. At first, I couldn't
calm down at all. My heart was pounding so hard I began
to worry about having a heart attack. Just as I would gain
control through deep breathing, the whole tent would
shake, as if the moose were bumping or nuzzling it, and
my heart would race again. Once, after an especially terri-
fying tremor, Nancy whispered, "I think it's lying down—I
feel something leaning against my leg, outside the tent."

What a terrible way to die, I thought. I could just picture the headline in the local paper: "Two Ohio Women
Squashed When 2,000-Pound Moose Rolls on Tent."

At first I prayed fervently for protection. Then, satisfied the Lord had heard me, and to get my mind off the

moose outside my fabric door, I began a Christian form of meditation—something health experts recommend as a powerful stress reducer. Silently, I started to recite every prayer and Scripture verse I could remember. Then I recalled my favorite songs of comfort and encouragement. This went on for hours.

> *Jesus, tender Shepherd, hear me,*
> *Bless Thy little lambs tonight.*
> *Through the darkness be Thou near me,*
> *Keep me safe 'til morning light.*

"The Lord is with me; I will not be afraid" (Psalm 118:6).

"God is our refuge and strength, an ever-present help in trouble" (Psalm 46:1).

> *Abide with me! Fast falls the eventide.*
> *The darkness deepens; Lord, with me abide!*
> *When other helpers fail and comforts flee,*
> *Help of the helpless, oh, abide with me!*
> —HENRY F. LYTE

My heart rate slowed. I could swallow again. And I was able to think straight.

My body's initial reaction would have come in handy if I were trying to fight off a mugger or run from a killer. However, the stress-produced chemicals causing those physical reactions were actually hurting me, and only by calming down did I slow their flow.

At daybreak, the moose nosed around our tent some more and then headed away from the campsite. We soon heard splashing in the nearby lake and realized it had gone to feed. We jumped up, quickly gathered our gear, and ran back up the trail toward safety.

I have often thought back to that night when I *did* "pray without ceasing" (1 Thessalonians 5:17, KJV). Later, through less physically dangerous but more emotionally upsetting experiences such as the trauma of a broken romance and the tragic death of someone I dearly loved, I again sought the soothing effect of those hopes and promises of my favorite old prayers, Scripture, and songs. When I could do nothing to change a situation, such meditation helped calm me and hastened physical as well as spiritual healing.

You really can worry yourself sick if you're not careful; doctors, counselors, and even the dictionary agree on that. Here's what *Webster's Third New International Dictionary* says:

STRESS: *A physical, chemical, or emotional factor to which an individual fails to make a satisfactory adaptation, and which causes physiologic tensions that may be a contributory cause of disease.*

Fear, irritability, tenseness, exhaustion, anger, and the feeling of being controlled by your commitments are all common symptoms of stress. Any major readjustment in life, good or bad, creates stress in the body, which causes a distinct physical and chemical reaction. Everyone faces stress.

Many things can cause bad stress. Single adults might feel the stress of the constant need for self-reliance. Married adults sometimes feel a loss of freedom, because there's always another person involved in decisions. Single parents raise their children alone; some feel helpless if the other parent gains custody. Parents of very young children might have different stresses, among them feeling isolated, overwhelmed, or fearful. Then there are the unexpected, dramatic events that happen without warning.

Even too many good experiences can hurt you. A promotion, a new marriage, a time-consuming job that you love, a move to a bigger house, a baby—all require physical and emotional adjustments, which create stress on the body.

What Stress Does to Your Body

The latest medical reports on the topic are frightening on one hand, and encouraging on the other.

First the frightening. Stress can kill. It does this by releasing a flood of hormones to the arteries, which, if left unchecked for too long, cause heart, liver, and circulatory damage.

The good news is that, with determination and effort, you can reverse the ill effects on your body and your mind. *Newsweek* magazine reported a medical study proving that heart disease can be reversed through a healthier lifestyle—one which includes meditating on a favorite short scripture or a line from a prayer or song.[1]

What happens, basically, is that when stress is caused by danger, excitement, anger, pain, depression, and many other events or emotions, the brain prepares the body for the famous "fight or flight" reaction. The pituitary gland releases hormones into the blood, which causes the adrenal glands to release a variety of natural chemicals. Each chemical has a purpose—some increase your energy and strength, some increase your heart rate, and some raise your blood pressure. Your body is literally flooded with hormones that create an unnaturally strong and alert state.

Your heart is the organ most often seriously damaged by too much stress. That's because it responds immediately to your moods, your physical activity, your positive and negative experiences, and is directly affected by the hormones released when you are under stress. Of the nearly

250 million Americans (1990), over 18 million have chronic heart disease. This is the leading cause of death in our country.[2] This sobering statistic could be reduced if more people took stress control more seriously.

Other side effects of stress include high blood pressure, muscle spasms, gastrointestinal problems, headaches, strokes, kidney disorders, damage to blood vessels of the eyes, anxiety, depression, and emotional disturbances.

How to Recognize Stress

To get some idea of how much stress you are under, and how you are handling it, take one of the widely accepted stress tests (such as those at the end of this chapter).

Dave, a 32-year-old businessman, sat near me on a recent trip. He made the mistake of asking me what I was working on, and then he heard more about stress than he really wanted to know. At my urging, he took the "Life-Event Test" (p. 15) and added up all the major events he had faced during the past year. Dave had moved to a different home, bought a new car, lost his job, started a new one, and experienced a painful divorce. On the Holmes-Rahe Social Readjustment Scale his score was 292, which meant he had an 80 percent chance of getting sick soon.

Based on my status as the train's resident stress expert, I prescribed more vegetables, fewer fatty foods, and more prayer, devotions, and exercise. Dave said he'd consider it. (But later at lunch, he left his broccoli and ate the roast beef. Comfortable habits die hard.)

Lynn, a teacher I have known for several years, was frustrated because her workday was made up of too many deadlines. She also frequently overate in reaction to tension, had indigestion, and couldn't concentrate on her work because she was always thinking about other obligations. She wasn't even aware of these feelings until she took the

"Simple Stress and Tension Test" (p. 17). She found she was a hot reactor and had trouble coping with everyday stress. Left unchanged, this behavior could seriously damage her cardiovascular system.

Long-term situations such as Lynn's can actually do the most damage. A onetime dangerous or dramatic experience may be extremely stressful but won't usually cause lasting damage. But when the stress or bad attitude drags on, so does the state of chemical arousal. When you see no relief in sight, your body stores up the stress-induced chemicals, and they end up turning on you.

Your temperament, experiences, physical health, personal habits, and other factors help determine how you cope with a stressful situation. The key to healthy coping is to learn the difference between good stress and bad stress, and where to draw the line with the amount of stress you willingly let into your life.

My friend Carol, a television journalist, is a delightful, highly visible Christian in great demand as a speaker at church dinners and other functions. For years, she pushed herself, sometimes agreeing to speak as often as seven times in one week. In addition, she worked full-time at a demanding job, always strove to be at her best in public, and tried to make time for her husband. She didn't take time out for vacations, and her adrenaline rarely stopped flowing.

Then came the night a few years ago when she returned home from work and fell in a heap, sobbing uncontrollably by her front door. She said she wasn't going back to work, didn't care about her job, and didn't want to do public speaking anymore. Her husband picked her up as if she were a child and put her to bed. When her condition hadn't improved the next morning, he called a doctor and drove her to his office. Still, she couldn't quit sobbing.

The diagnosis: too much stress, which had triggered a serious anxiety disorder. The doctor prescribed complete rest for several weeks. After that, Carol was to cut back on future speaking engagements. The doctor also recommended immediate but temporary use of an antianxiety medication to stop her physical and emotional turmoil. Within a few weeks, she felt better and was able to return to work. She eventually learned to control her anxiety through diet, exercise, more liberal use of the word *no*, and deliberately releasing her job and her commitments to the Lord.

"I know that this job could disappear in a moment," she says. "I could get sick or get fired. The only thing that is secure in this life is Jesus Christ."

Although the doctor's order to cut back on the speaking engagements was initially stressful in itself, since it produced guilt, Carol learned the hard way how to respect her body. "I now know that there are other Christians out there who can speak just as well, probably better, than I can," she says now. "I finally realized that it wasn't my responsibility to speak at every single mother-daughter banquet or Christian school fund-raiser in the city. We each have to guard our time and energy."

The same stress that had helped Carol in her work by giving her the energy to thoroughly cover news and perform well on the air was wrecking her personal life and destroying her health. When she finally learned to control the stress, her health improved.

How to Reduce the Stress

If you, like Carol, are an overachiever who loves what you do but don't know when to quit, ask yourself if someone else could do some of the extra things you take on. Perhaps, by refusing to take on too many commitments, you would be giving others more opportunities to contribute. Some people have a lot to give but rarely get asked to help.

Perhaps, like Dave, you have had an unusually stressful year due to events beyond your control. You need to realize that the stress may have weakened your immune system, making you more prone to illness. You can't undo what was done, but you can strengthen your immune system through a low-fat diet, rest, exercise, soothing music, and prayer.

If you're a hot reactor, like Lynn, you've got a bigger challenge. You need to exercise, rest, pray, and watch your diet. But you also have to learn to change your attitude and reaction patterns. This "bad stress" distresses you and isn't improving your work performance. Instead, it makes you miserable.

One effective way to immediately reduce stress and anxiety is to breathe slowly and deeply. Fast, shallow breathing increases stress. But by controlling your breathing, especially during spiritual meditation and prayer, you can immediately begin to relieve some of the stress on your body.

Many Christians have known for years that prayerful meditation is an effective antidote to the stress of living in a sinful world. Now, even secular medical experts are noting that prayer and praise, comforting inspirational music, Christian fellowship groups, and devotional meditation are powerful stress reducers.

For a longer, healthier life, we all need to recognize the symptoms of stress, eat a healthy diet, exercise moderately, pick our fights carefully, avoid moose-filled campsites, and learn when to use the word no.

I also find it helpful to relax for at least 10 minutes once or twice a day, using controlled breathing and prayer.

You may be surprised at what happens to your spirit in the process of taking better care of your body.

One more thing:

"Rejoice in the Lord always. I will say it again: Rejoice! Let your gentleness be evident to all. The Lord is near. Do not be anxious about anything, but in everything, by prayer and petition, with thanksgiving, present your requests to God. And the peace of God, which transcends all understanding, will guard your hearts and your minds in Christ Jesus. Finally, brothers, whatever is true, whatever is noble, whatever is right, whatever is pure, whatever is lovely, whatever is admirable—if anything is excellent or praiseworthy—think about such things" (Philippians 4:4-8).

---

1. L. Shapiro, "A New Menu to Heal the Heart," *Newsweek*, July 30, 1990, 58-59.

2. Source: National Center for Health Statistics.

BACKGROUND SCRIPTURE: *Philippians 4:4-8*

Vicki Hesterman is associate professor of journalism, Point Loma Nazarene College, San Diego. She is also a free-lance writer and author of two books. Copyright 1992 Vicki Hesterman.

Life-Event Test

You can explore the stress in your life by finding out how many changes you've faced recently. This test contains a list of some events that commonly occur in life. Check the left-hand column if the event has happened to you during the last 12 months.

LIFE EVENT	POINTS
_____ Death of spouse	100
_____ Divorce	73
_____ Marital separation	65
_____ Jail term	63
_____ Death of close family member	63
_____ Personal injury or illness	53
_____ Marriage	50
_____ Fired at work	47
_____ Marital reconciliation	45
_____ Retirement	45
✓✗ Change in family member's health	44
✓ Pregnancy	40
_____ Sex difficulties	39
✓✗ Addition to family	39
_____ Business readjustment	39
_____ Change in financial state	38
✓ Death of close friend	37
✗ Change to different line of work	36
_____ Change in number of marital arguments	35
_____ Mortgage or loan for major purchase (home, etc.)	31
_____ Foreclosure of mortgage or loan	30
✓✗ Change in work responsibilities	29
_____ Son or daughter leaving home	29
_____ Trouble with in-laws	29
_____ Outstanding personal achievement	28
_____ Spouse begins or stops work	26
_____ Starting or finishing school	26

_____	Change in living conditions	25
_____	Revision of personal habits	24
_____	Trouble with boss	23
_✓X_	Change in work hours, conditions	20
_____	Change in residence	20
_____	Change in schools	20
_____	Change in recreational activities	19
_✓X_	Change in church activities	19
_____	Change in social activities	18
_____	Mortgage or loan for lesser purchase (car, TV, etc.)	17
_✓X_	Change in sleeping habits	16
_____	Change in number of family gatherings	15
_____	Change in eating habits	15
_____	Vacation	13
_✓X_	Christmas season	12
_____	Minor violation of the law	11

Total score: 250/179

Now, add up the point values of all the items checked. If your score is 300 or more, statistically you stand an almost 80 percent chance of getting sick in the near future. If your score is 150 to 299, the chances are about 50 percent. At less than 150, about 30 percent.

Dani – 250
Billy – 179

Reprinted by permission from the *Journal of Psychosomatic Research*, vol. 11, Thomas H. Holmes and Richard R. Rahe, "The Social Readjustment Rating Scale," © 1967, Pergamon Press.

Simple Stress and Tension Test

This test helps assess how you are living. The questions are not weighted for relative importance; they are meant to give you a general idea of how you are doing and to alert you to some signs and sources of stress in your life.

	Often	A few times a week	Rarely
1. I feel tense, anxious, or have nervous indigestion.	2	1	0
2. People at work/home arouse my tension.	2	1	0
3. I eat/drink/smoke in response to tension.	2	1	0
4. I have tension or migraine headaches, pain in the neck or shoulders, or insomnia.	2	1	0
5. I can't turn off my thoughts at night or on weekends long enough to feel relaxed and refreshed the next day.	2	1	0
6. I find it difficult to concentrate on what I'm doing because of worrying about other things.	2	1	0
7. I take tranquilizers (or other drugs) to relax.	2	1	0
8. I have a difficult time finding enough time to relax.	2	1	0
9. Once I find the time, it's hard for me to relax.	Yes (1)		No (0)
10. My workday is made up of too many deadlines.	Yes (1)		No (0)

Total score: _____

A score of 12 or higher indicates a high tension level and difficulty coping with the stress in your life.

Source: John W. Farquhar, M.D., *The American Way of Life Need Not Be Hazardous to Your Health* (New York: W. W. Norton Co., 1979). Reprinted by permission of the publisher. Copyright 1978 by John W. Farquhar, M.D.

2

Driven People
Caught in a Golden Cage

*They're Not Nice,
but They Get the Job Done*

by Gordon MacDonald

THE 12 MEN who followed Jesus Christ and ultimately founded His Church were a strange group. There is not one of them (with the possible exception of John, whom I find to be likable and nonthreatening) I would have picked to lead a movement of the proportions of Christ's mission. But Jesus called them, and you know the result.

Frankly, some of those volunteers who were turned down by Jesus are more my style. They were go-getters; they knew a good thing when they saw it. They seem to have been bursting with enthusiasm. And He turned them down! Why?

Perhaps Jesus, with His extraordinary insight, looked into their private worlds and saw danger signs. Perhaps He saw *driven men,* out to make something of themselves. Maybe the very thing I like about them was the problem: they wanted to control the situation by saying when they would start and where they would go.

Today, there are lots of driven people doing very good things. Driven people are not necessarily bad folk, although the consequences of their drivenness may produce unfortunate results. In fact, driven people often make great contributions. They start organizations; they provide jobs and opportunities; they are often very bright and offer ways of doing things that benefit many other people. But nevertheless they are driven, and one worries about their ability to sustain the pace without danger to themselves.

Can driven people be spotted? Yes, of course. There are many symptoms that suggest a person is driven. Among the ones I see most often are these:

1. A driven person is most often gratified only by accomplishment. Somewhere in the process of maturation this person discovers that the only way he can feel good about himself and his world is to accumulate accomplishments. This discovery may be the result of formative influences at an early age; as a child, affirmation and approval may have been received from a parent or influential mentor only when something had been finished. Nothing of value may have ever been said until that task was completed. Thus the only way he could find love and acceptance was through accomplishment.

A psychology of achievement sometimes captures the heart in circumstances like that. A person begins to reason that if one accomplishment resulted in good feelings and the praise of others, then several more accomplishments may bring an abundance of good feelings and affirmations.

So the driven person begins to look for ways to accumulate more and more achievements. He will soon be found doing two or three things at one time, because that brings even more of this strange sort of pleasure. He becomes the sort of person who is always reading books and attending seminars that promise to help him use what time he has even more effectively. Why? So he can produce more accomplishments, which in turn will provide greater gratification.

This is the kind of person who sees life only in terms of results. As such he has little appreciation for the *process* leading toward results. This kind of person would love to fly from New York to Los Angeles at supersonic speed because to travel at ground speed and see the hills of Pennsylvania, the golden wheat of Iowa and Nebraska, the awesomeness of the Rockies, and the deserts of Utah and Nevada would be a terrible waste of time. Upon arrival in Los Angeles after a swift two-hour trip, this driven person would be highly irritated if the plane took four extra minutes to get into the gate. Arrival is everything to this accomplishment-oriented individual; the trip means nothing.

2. A driven person is preoccupied with the symbols of accomplishment. He is usually conscious of the concept of power, and he seeks to possess it in order to wield it. That means he will be aware of the symbols of status: titles, office size and location, positions on organizational charts, and special privileges.

There is generally a concern for one's own notoriety when in a state of drivenness. Who, the driven person wonders, knows about what I am doing? How can I be better connected with the "greats" of my world? These questions often preoccupy the driven person.

3. A driven person is usually caught in the uncontrolled pursuit of expansion. Driven people like to be a part of something that is getting bigger and more successful. They are usually on the move, seeking the biggest and the best opportunities. They rarely have any time to appreciate the achievements to date.

The 19th-century English preacher Charles Spurgeon once said:

> Success exposes a man to the pressures of people and thus tempts him to hold on to his gains by means of fleshly methods and practices, and to let himself be ruled wholly by the dictatorial demands of incessant expansion. Success can go to my head and will unless I remember that it is God who accomplishes the work, that He can continue to do so without my help, and that He will be able to make out with other means whenever He wants to cut me out.*

You can see this unfortunate principle in the pursuit of some careers. But you can also see it in the context of spiritual activity, for there is such a thing as a spiritually driven person who is never satisfied with who he is or what he accomplishes in religious work. And of course this means that his attitude toward those around him is much the same. He is rarely pleased with the progress of his peers or subordinates. He lives in a constant state of uneasiness and restlessness, looking for more efficient methods, greater results, deeper spiritual experiences. There is usually no sign he will ever be satisfied with himself or anyone else.

4. Driven people tend to have a limited regard for integrity. They can become so preoccupied with success and achievement that they have little time to stop and ask if their inner person is keeping pace with the outer process. Usually it is not, and there is an increasing gap, a breakdown in integrity.

People like this often become progressively deceitful; and they not only deceive others, they deceive themselves. In the attempt to push ahead relentlessly, they lie to themselves about motives; values and morals are compromised. Shortcuts to success become a way of life. Because the goal is so important, they drift into ethical shabbiness. Driven people become frighteningly pragmatic.

5. Driven people often possess limited or undeveloped people skills. They are not noted for getting along well with others. Projects are more important to them than people. Because their eyes are upon goals, they rarely take note of the people about them, unless they can be used for the fulfillment of one of the goals. And if others are not found to be useful, then they may be seen as obstacles or competitors when it comes to getting something done.

There is usually a "trail of bodies" in the wake of the driven person. Where once others praised him for his seemingly great leadership, there soon appears a steady increase in frustration and hostility, as they see that the driven person cares very little about the health and growth of human beings. It becomes apparent that there is a nonnegotiable agenda, and it is supreme above all other things. Colleagues and subordinates in the orbit of the driven person slowly drop away, one after another, exhausted, exploited, and disillusioned.

Of this person we are most likely to find ourselves saying, "He is miserable to work with, but he certainly gets things done."

And therein lies the rub. He gets things done, but he may destroy people in the process. Not an attractive sight. Yet the ironic thing, which cannot be ignored, is that in almost every great organization, religious and secular, people of this sort can be found in key positions. Even though they carry with them the seeds of relational disaster, they often are indispensable to the action.

6. Driven people tend to be highly competitive. They see each effort as a win-or-lose game. And, of course, the driven person feels he must win, must look good before others. The more driven he is, the larger the score by which he needs to win.

Winning provides the evidence the driven person desperately needs that he is right, valuable, and important. Thus, he is likely to see others as competitors or as enemies who must be beaten—perhaps even humiliated—in the process.

7. A driven person often possesses a volcanic force of anger. And it can erupt any time he senses opposition or disloyalty. This anger can be triggered when people disagree, offer an alternative solution to a problem, or even hint at just a bit of criticism.

The anger may not surface as physical violence. But it can take the form of verbal brutality: profanity or humiliating insults, for example. The anger can express itself in vindictive acts such as firing people, slandering them before peers, or simply denying them things they have come to expect, such as affection, money, or even companionship.

A close friend tells of sitting in an office with several working associates while the office manager, a woman who had worked for the company for 15 years, made a plea for a week off to be with a sick baby. She made the mistake of responding tearfully when the boss refused her request. When he turned and saw her tears, he snarled, "Clean out your desk and get out of here; I don't need you anyhow." When she was gone, he turned to the horrified onlookers and said, "Let's get one thing straight; you're all here for only one reason: to make me money. And if you don't like it, get out right now!"

Tragically, many good people who surround the driven person are more than willing to take the impact of such anger, although it desperately hurts them, because they reason that the boss or the leader is getting things done, that he is being blessed by God, or that no one can argue with success. Sometimes the anger and its cruel effects are accepted simply because no one has either the courage or the ability to stand up to the driven person.

Recently a person who serves on the board of a major Christian organization told me of encounters with the executive director that included outbursts of anger studded with extraordinary profanity and demeaning language. When I asked why board members accepted this form of behavior, which was neither rare nor open to excuse, he said, "I guess we were so impressed with the way that God seemed to use him in his public ministry that we were reluctant to confront."

Is there anything else worth saying about the driven person, who by now appears to be entirely unlikable? Yes, simply this:

8. Driven people are usually abnormally busy. They are usually too busy for the pursuit of ordinary relationships in marriage, family, or friendship, or even to carry on a relationship with themselves—not to speak of one with God. Because driven people rarely think they have accomplished enough, they seize every available minute to attend more meetings, to study more material, to initiate more projects. They operate on the precept that a reputation for busyness is a sign of success and personal importance. Thus they attempt to impress people with the fullness of the schedule. They may even express a high level of self-pity, bemoaning the "trap" of responsibility they claim to be in, wishing aloud that there was some possible release from all that they have to live with. But just try to suggest a way out.

The truth is that the very worst thing that could happen to them would be if someone provided them with a way out. They really wouldn't know what to do with themselves if there were suddenly less to do. Busyness for the driven person becomes a habit, a way of life and thought. They find it enjoyable to complain and gather pity, and they would probably not want it any different. But tell a driven person that, and you'll make him angry.

This then is the driven person—not an entirely attractive picture. What often disturbs me as I look at this picture is the fact that much of our world is run by driven people. We have created a system that rides on their backs. In businesses, in churches, and in homes, the growth of people is often sacrificed for accomplishment and accumulation.

Pastors who are driven men have been known to burn out scores of assistants and lay leaders because of their need to head organizations that are the biggest, the best, and the most well-known. There are businesspeople who claim Christian faith and who have enjoyed a reputation for graciousness in the church, but who are ruthless in the office, pushing people and squeezing them for the last ounce of energy simply so that they themselves can enjoy the gratification of winning, accumulating, or establishing a reputation.

Recently a businessman became a Christian through the witness of a layman who is a good friend of mine. Not long after making his choice to follow Jesus Christ, he wrote a long letter to my friend who had guided him into faith. In it he described some of his struggles as the result of his driven condition. I requested permission to share part of the letter because it so vividly illustrated the driven person. He wrote:

> Several years ago I was at a point of great frustration in my life. Although I had a wonderful wife and three beautiful sons, my career was going badly. I had few friends, my oldest son began getting into trouble—he started failing in school—I was suffering from depression, there was great tension and unhappiness in my family. At that time I had an opportunity to travel overseas where I stayed to work in a foreign company. This new opportunity was such an excellent one, financially and career-wise, that I made it number one in my life, forsaking all other values. I did many wrong (i.e., sinful) things to advance my position and success. I justified them as being of good consequence to my family (more money, etc.)—resulted in my lying to myself and my family and behaving wrongly in many ways.
>
> Of course this was intolerable to my wife, and she and my family returned to the U.S. I was still blind, however, to the problems that were within me. My success, my salary, my career—all moved upward. I *was caught in a golden cage* . . . [italics mine]
>
> Although many wonderful things were happening outside me, inside I was losing everything. My capacity to reason and my capacity to decide were both weakened. I would evaluate alternatives, constantly going over various options, always trying to pick the one that would maximize success and career. I knew in my heart that something was terribly wrong. I went to church, but the words there couldn't reach me. I was too caught up in my own world.
>
> After a terrible episode with my family several weeks ago, I completely gave up my course of thinking and went to a hotel room for nine days to figure out what to do. The more I thought, the more troubled I became. I began to realize how dead I really was, how so much of my life was dark. And worse than that, I could see no way out. My only solu-

tion was to run and hide, to start in a different place, to sever all connections.

This brutal description of a man on the bottom fortunately has a happy ending. For not long after his nine-day experience in a hotel room, he discovered the love of God and its capacity to engender dramatic change in his life. He got out of his golden cage.

In the Bible few men typify the driven man better than Saul, the first king of Israel. Unlike the previous story, this story has a miserable ending, for Saul never got out of his golden cage. All he did was heap increasing amounts of stress upon himself. And it destroyed him.

The Bible's introduction to Saul should be warning enough that the man had some flaws that, if not addressed within his inner world, would cause him quickly to lose personal control.

> Now there was a man of Benjamin whose name was Kish the son of Abiel, the son of Zeror, the son of Becorath, the son of Aphiah, the son of a Benjamite, a mighty man of valor. And he had a son whose name was Saul, a choice and handsome man, and there was not a more handsome person than he among the sons of Israel; from his shoulders and up he was taller than any of the people *(1 Samuel 9:1-2, NASB).*

Saul possessed three unearned characteristics at the beginning of his public life that had the potential to become assets or serious liabilities. Which they would be was his choice. And how Saul made those choices depended upon the daily order of his private world.

The three? First, wealth; second, an attractive appearance; and third, a physically large and well-developed body.

All three external marks commanded attention and gained him quick advantages. (Each time I think of Saul's natural gifts, I recall the bank president some years ago who said to me, "MacDonald, you could go a long way in the business world if you were about six inches taller.") And, most importantly, they provided him with a sort of charisma that made possible his achieving some early success without ever having to develop a heart of wisdom or spiritual stature. He was simply a fast starter.

As Saul's story unfolds in the biblical text, we learn some other things about the man, things that could have either contributed to his success or become a part of his ultimate failure. We are told, for example, that he was good with words. When he was given a chance to speak before crowds, he was eloquent. The stage was set for a man to consolidate power and command recognition without ever having to develop any sense of a strong inner world first. And that was where the danger lay.

When Saul became king of Israel, he enjoyed too much immediate success. It apparently made him unaware that he had any limits to his life. He spent little time pondering his need for others, engendering a relationship with God, or even facing his responsibilities toward the people over whom he ruled. The signs of a driven man began to appear.

Saul became a busy man; he saw worlds he thought needed conquering. Thus when he faced an impending battle with the Philistines, Israel's great enemy of the day, and waited at Gilgal for Samuel the prophet to come and offer the necessary sacrifices, he grew impatient and irritable when the holy man did not arrive on time. Saul felt that his timetable was being compromised; he had to get on with things. His remedy? Offer the sacrifice himself. And that is exactly what he did.

The result? A rather serious breach of covenant with God. Offering sacrifice was the kind of thing prophets like

Samuel did, not kings like Saul. But Saul had forgotten that because he saw himself as being too important.

From that time forward Saul found himself on a downhill track. "But now your kingdom will not endure; the Lord has sought out a man after his own heart" (1 Samuel 13:14a). This is how most driven men end.

Stripped of what blessing and assistance he had had from God up to this point, Saul's drivenness began to reveal itself even further. Soon all of his energies became consumed in holding onto his throne, competing with young David, who had caught the imagination of the people of Israel.

The Scriptures give several examples of Saul's explosive anger, which drove him to outrage as well as to moments of paralyzing self-pity. By the end of his life, he was a man out of control, seeing enemies behind every bush. Why? Because from the very beginning Saul had been a driven man, and he never came to grips with his drivenness by simply facing the inner rebukes God would have liked for him to have heard.

Saul would not have lasted long among the 12 disciples Jesus picked. His own compulsions were far too strong. That which had driven him to grasp power and not let go, that which had caused him to turn on his closest supporters, and that which caused him to make a successive series of unwise decisions, finally led him to a humiliating death. He was the classic driven man.

To the extent that we see him in ourselves, we have work to do in our private worlds. For an inner life fraught with unresolved drives will not be able to hear clearly the voice of Christ when He calls. The noise and pain of stress will be too great.

Unfortunately, our society abounds with Sauls, men and women caught in golden cages, driven to accumulate, to be recognized, or to achieve. Our churches, unfortunately, abound with these driven people as well. Many churches are fountains gone dry. Rather than being springs of life-giving energy that cause people to grow and to delight in God's way, they become sources of stress. The driven man's private world is disordered. His cage may be lavishly golden. But it's a trap; inside there is nothing that lasts.

---

*Cited in J. Oswald Sanders, *Spiritual Leadership* (Chicago: Moody Press, 1967), 23.

BACKGROUND SCRIPTURE: Ephesians 2:4-10; 4:1-3

Gordon MacDonald is a pastor in New York City. This chapter is reprinted by permission from *Ordering Your Private World*, by Gordon MacDonald, © 1985 Oliver-Nelson Publishers.

3

The Whole Country Is Changing

*It's Getting Darker Skin,
Grayer Hair,
and Bone-Tired Busy*

by Leith Anderson

CHANGING TIMES magazine changed its name to *Kiplinger's Personal Finance Magazine.* It is one more reminder that our society is being swamped by changes when even the change magazines change.

The changes are happening around the world. The interest rates in Germany and Japan influence how much we pay for a car loan. Democracy has spread from America to East Germany to Russia. Cities are growing by millions, while rural areas are slowly dying as people move away. The list could go on and on, but let's look at some of the important changes happening here at home.

People on the Move

My mother was born in northern England and emigrated to the United States as an adult. My father, the grandson of Swedish immigrants, was born and raised in Camden, N.J. Though my wife, Charleen, and I grew up in neighboring towns in New Jersey, we went away to college in Illinois and have not lived within a thousand miles of our immediate families since. We have extended family in Florida, Illinois, California, Pennsylvania, Connecticut, and Texas. Some of our friends have changed addresses so many times our address book doesn't have room for another listing.

When parents, grandparents, and grandchildren are thousands of miles apart, extended families no longer share child-rearing responsibilities. Traditional values that were reinforced in small towns and neighborhoods often disappear in a community of newcomers and strangers.

Though mobility is mostly a matter of physical location, it is also a mentality. Movement in society creates an openness to mobility in jobs and relationships and churches. Just as we move from city to city or house to house, we may also move from marriage to marriage and job to job.

Even our cars are changing to show our mobility. We commute farther, so cars have turned into living rooms with fancy sound systems, telephones, and adjustable seating. One popular minivan boasts 14 separate cup holders but seats eight people. Just right for all the trips to the fast-food drive-through.

The Color of a Nation

The white population of the United States isn't growing, but it is aging. The "minority" population (including African Americans, Native Americans, Asian Americans, and Hispanics) is growing larger in number and younger in age.

This coloring of America is a result of both immigration and high birthrate. And the impact is greater in some parts of the country than others. California, for example, is projecting that whites will soon be a minority.

The enormous tension facing our society, and especially our churches, is how to justly assimilate persons of color and still encourage ethnic identity. Many whites have traditionally considered minorities a threat rather than an opportunity, both in the community and in the church.

More Gray Hair

For the first time in our history, there are more Americans over 65 than there are teenagers. The over-65 senior citizen group has increased 50 percent since 1950, and it will increase another 75 percent over the next four decades as baby boomers (born from 1946 to 1964) move into retirement.

At the same time, the youth population is shrinking. During the 1990s the 18 to 25 age-group is expected to decrease by 12 percent. In 1980, for example, there were 4.2 million 19-year-olds; now there are about 3.1 million. The fastest-growing age-group in America is the age-group over 85. By 1998 the number of Americans over 85 will have grown by 50 percent. At the same time there will be a 45 percent increase in 45 to 50-year-olds and a 21 percent increase in those 75 to 84.

You don't have to read the statistics to see the graying of America. Just watch your TV. There were three men in their 90s who ran in the 1990 New York Marathon. Two of them finished. We not only have more older people but more active older people.

Since older people tend to control money and cast more votes, they have a big influence on our society, and they are changing it very quickly. Public policy favors keeping Social Security benefits increasing while decreasing aid to college students. The national debt has mushroomed in size—it is buying for today's older people and leaving the payments for the younger people.

Working Women

Women have always worked. Before World War II, when America had a more agricultural economy, most worked at home or on the family farm. During the war women entered the commercial work force in increased numbers to alleviate the domestic manpower shortage. After the war, what had begun as a military and industrial necessity for the nation became an economic necessity for the American family.

Today 50 percent of American women work outside the home, and the Labor Department estimates that the figure will rise to 61 percent. While many are employed out of economic need, many see work as the pursuit of a career. Women make up 20 percent of America's physicians, twice the proportion of 1970, and one-third of the current medical school students are women. Increasingly, women are entering, if not leading, fields traditionally dominated by men.

This change in American society has had and will continue to exert great influence on the church. In the past women have been the bulk of volunteers for churches, school activities, and community service. This is no longer possible. Women who work are not available during the day, and when they come home, they are occupied with traditional household responsibilities. Many are also single mothers who may themselves be in great need of those services conducted by volunteers. What some older church leaders think is a declining commitment is really busyness, family responsibilities, and just plain tiredness.

Mind-boggling Choices

Just a generation ago there were only three television networks, three major automobile manufacturers, few medical specialists, identical interest rates at all banks, and the same fares on every airline. Magazine racks at the corner drugstore carried a limited selection of periodicals such as *Time, Life, Look,* and the *Saturday Evening Post.*

Today the choices are mind-boggling. Airline fares change thousands of times every month as computer programs constantly adjust to fares posted by competing carriers. Every bank has a different interest rate depending on the amount of deposit and term of investment. Magazines are highly specialized, with separate publications for everything from computers (specialized by type), to skiing (downhill or cross-country), to soap operas. Televisions come with 110-channel capability, and many parts of the country have cable choices ranging from sports to pornography, from English to Spanish, from opera to rock and roll, from 24-hour weather reports to 24-hour news channels.

Choices add stress. Every decision makes life a bit more complicated. It can take days to comparison shop all the models and prices of timesaving appliances. Even going to McDonald's has become more stressful with the increased choices on the menu.

Businesses have figured out that some people are more likely to buy their products than others. So they have "segmented" society to target their advertising. Diapers and other baby products are advertised in magazines and on TV shows that appeal to young mothers. Since Cadillacs tend to be purchased by older drivers, they are advertised at times and places that will get the attention of older people.

Nowhere is the stress of choices more obvious than when tuning a radio in a metropolitan area. There are stations just for the young, the old, those who like classical music and those who like contemporary music, those who speak English or Korean or Spanish, those who like news and those who hate the news. One Florida station now broadcasts only commercials—for those who like ads.

Short-term Commitments

Modern American society places great emphasis on self, independence, and personal fulfillment. Combined with mobility and uncertainty, these trends make long-term commitments seem inappropriate.

When rapid change appears to be the norm, people are reluctant to commit to anything. Unlike the Japanese, who tend to spend their entire lives working for one employer, most Americans change jobs several times. This may be out of economic necessity or for career advancement. Or it may be the result of mergers, corporate takeovers, or changing economics that reduce or remove an industry from the scene. A generation ago corporate giants hired at good wages with great benefits. Now they are laying off and reducing benefits. Cheryl Russell, editor of *American Demographics* magazine, estimates baby boomers will work at 10 different jobs during their lifetime. On the average, workers now change careers three times in their lives. Workers are less committed to companies, and companies are less committed to workers.

More marriages ended in divorce during the 1970s and 1980s than during any other period of American history.

Not only has this stamped divorce as socially acceptable, it has also created a generation of children who have experienced divorce, single-parent homes, and multiple marriages as the norm rather than the exception. Though most couples entering marriage would say they are making a lifetime commitment, they know divorce is a possibility if either or both are dissatisfied. This varies greatly from their grandparents' generation (and the laws of their grandparents' generation), which seldom saw divorce as an option.

Regardless of the "why" of short-term commitments, the frequency is easily observed. Fewer people are interested in joining clubs, taking on assignments, signing contracts, or doing anything that will reduce the options for future choices.

How Should We Respond?

Some will say these stresses from society are too much to expect people to cope with. Just reading the list adds to the depression. Others respond with 87 more additions to the list. No doubt, the stresses are many more than I've covered in this brief discussion.

The question is "how should a Christian respond?" Do we not have a different perspective because of our personal relationship with Jesus Christ?

1. Be aware. Christians should not put their heads in the sand. We should be aware of what is happening in the society around us.

Our models include Moses, who mastered the Egyptian culture without forsaking his Hebrew heritage; Paul, who quoted a heathen Greek poet as he preached to the people gathered at Mars' Hill in Athens; and Jesus, who came from heaven to know and reach society for salvation.

Let's read the newspaper, watch the television news,

and observe what is going on around us. Not to adopt society's standards but to be aware of the world God loves.

2. Keep the faith. There is never a need to doubt God's final control over everything that happens in this world. He is never caught by surprise. God is never outmaneuvered by any modern trend. God is never weakened by stress.

Our Lord is the God of history who knows the end from the beginning and really does work everything together for good (Romans 8:28).

It is true the changes in society can stress us, but they can also stretch and strengthen us. The biggest issue is not what is happening but how we respond. An important Christian response is to trust God.

3. Take opportunity. History teaches us that some of the best times to convince others to become Christians are during the stress periods. During wars, famines, natural disasters, and social upheavals, more people are open to the gospel of Jesus Christ than during times of less stress and greater peace.

Right now is one of our grandest opportunities to present the peace of Jesus Christ to stressed-out Americans.

In recent years the hurricane forces of change have dramatically altered our societal landscape. The changes are breathtaking, and some skeptics wonder if the Church and Christianity can survive.

Let there be no doubt—the cause and Church of Jesus Christ will not only survive but thrive.

Jesus was and is the greatest change agent in the universe. The Incarnation was and is the greatest union of revelation and relevance ("The Word became flesh and made his dwelling among us," John 1:14). Jesus changes sinners into saints—the ultimate human transformation. He then develops those saints into the Church, "and the gates of Hades will not overcome it" (Matthew 16:18).

As the 20th century ends and the 21st century begins, Christians are privileged to see God perform His great acts through us and Christ's Church one more time.

BACKGROUND SCRIPTURE: *Matthew 16:18; Romans 8:28*

Leith Anderson is senior pastor of Wooddale Church, Eden Prairie, Minn., and author of *Dying for Change* (Bethany House Publishers), from which this chapter is adapted.

4

Wanted: Less Stress for Working Stiffs

Critical Boss, Boring Job?
Here's What You Can Do

by Randy Michael

LET ME TELL YOU about a couple I counseled. Actually, they are more than a couple. They are a composite of people I've worked with in my counseling practice.

I think you might just recognize the pair. At the very least, I think you'll sympathize with them and relate to the troubles they face because of their jobs.

It was morning in their house.

Marsha woke the children, while Scott gathered the cereal boxes and dishes from the shelves, the utensils from the drawer, and the glasses—no clean glasses! Rinsing would have to do.

Scott would take Nina to child care. Marsha would drop Jon at his friend's house so that they could walk to school together. Everyone slept in a little on this chilly morning, so Scott and Marsha would be lucky to make it to work on time.

As Scott dumped the breakfast cache on the table and reached for his 10-ounce beaker of coffee, he thought about the performance review he would face that morning. Would his boss be critical again? Scott had tried to improve his performance, but his supervisor was very demanding—too demanding, Scott thought.

An even more foreboding thought was what the recent company merger would mean to him. It had already meant extra work with no extra help and no extra pay. But would Scott even have a job after the dust settled?

As he thought about this, he could feel the muscles tighten in his neck, shoulder, and chest. Was he going to get another one of his tension headaches?

Just then Marsha rushed into the kitchen, shepherding a still-sleepy Jon and Nina. Scott excused himself to finish getting ready. Marsha was left alone with her two weary kids and her early-morning thoughts.

She had her own problems at work. Though Scott was grappling with major changes, her problem was just the opposite. Her office work had become routine and boring. As she settled in for a quick moment with a bowl of cereal, her mind wandered again to whether she should return to school. But with the uncertainty of Scott's job and with the children the ages they were, it seemed best to wait.

Marsha, who was more easygoing than Scott, usually felt less stressed-out than her husband. But this morning the stress of returning to a lifeless job settled into the pit of her stomach, then began slowly churning.

Scott and Marsha are like most of us: they experience work-related stress. And this stress doesn't stay at the office. It follows them home. Complicating things all the more, the stress of their personal life follows them to work.

How can they cope with this?

They need to do three things: (1) acquire an understanding of work stress; (2) recognize their own stress; and (3) take steps to lower their stress level.

Stress on the Job

Stress in the workplace, or anywhere else for that matter, comes from demands placed on us.

Scott is facing stress because:

- he overslept
- he faces a performance review
- he has a critical boss
- his company took part in a merger
- the merger means extra work
- he may lose his job

Marsha is stressed because:

- her job is boring
- she wants to upgrade her training but can't because of the uncertainty of Scott's job

Scott and Marsha experience their work-related stress in at least three different ways.

1. The first difference relates to the fact that what produces stress for one person might not produce stress for another.

For instance, Scott does not mind his half-hour commute to and from work. But Marsha gets tense about her 15-minute adrenaline jump-start on the rush-hour expressway.

On the other hand, Marsha does not take her performance reviews as hard as does Scott. She tries to learn from them but does not brood over them or let them undermine her sense of self-worth.

2. Another difference is that though Scott's neck, shoulder, and chest muscles get tense during stress, Marsha's stomach becomes tight.

3. Generally, Scott is more driven and competitive than Marsha. That increases his overall stress level.

So far, it's sounding like stress is a pretty bad thing to have—like a disease. But that's not so. Stress is part of life. We fantasize stress-free living, but that is unrealistic. We need to experience stress for stimulation. Stress-free living is boring (which in turn becomes stressful; ask folks like Marsha).

The distinction is that some stresses are experienced as *distress*—that which is uncomfortable, toxic, and over-whelming. But other stress is what psychologists call *eustress*—that which is positive, stimulating, and tension-relieving. Skydiving would be distress for some, but eu-stress for others. A quiet, structured work environment is needed by some people, while for others such a setting would produce unbearable distress.

Scott likes a quiet office. But since the merger, he has had to share an office. And there have been constant inter-ruptions. He experiences this as distress. Marsha, on the other hand, works in a secretarial pool and finds such a setting to be eustress for her.

Take a Stress Inventory

Once Scott and Marsha better understand the nature of stress on the job, they need to recognize their own stress. The symptoms are clearly there.

Scott's accuracy has been decreasing, and it has been more difficult for him to make decisions. With Marsha's boredom, she looks for things to do rather than letting work stack up. But she still is not as efficient as she has been, and her mind tends to wander.

Physiologically, Marsha and Scott respond differently. She is more ulcer prone; he, more prone to coronary heart disease. Both of them are organizationally less productive than they could be.

Psychologically, Scott has been more irritable both at work and at home. Marsha has been more apathetic. Marsha tends to keep her frustration to herself.

Scott and Marsha need to *choose* to become more aware of their stress symptoms. Such choosing is essential. But it's hard for them because they are caught up in their situation. Yet if they do not recognize their symptoms, not only will they continue on their current stress treadmill, but also its speed will increase. The result could be further deterioration of relationships, decreased job performance, and increased risk of physical breakdown through heart disease, headaches, ulcers, arthritis, and a host of other illnesses brought on or aggravated by stress.

This couple needs to set aside an hour or two, preferably on a weekend, and take a stress inventory. They need to chart their symptoms in the following categories.

Physical Condition
(sore muscles; tight stomach; headaches; shortness of breath; light-headedness; aching joints)

Psychological Condition
(irritability; feeling out of control; feeling an urge to cry; feeling anxious, tense, depressed, angry)

Behavioral Condition
(troubled relationships; poor job performance; compulsive behavior—eating, drinking, taking drugs other than according to physician's prescription; excessive time alone; lethargy)

Spiritual Condition

(a lack of: close, consistent relationship with God; a sense of peace growing out of being centered in the Lord; allowing the Lord to be a resource for life and living and doing one's work as unto Him rather than for others)

In addition to taking this kind of personal inventory, it would be wise for Marsha and Scott to have physical checkups. Stress has a profound impact on one's body. Monitoring of this is an important part of being good stewards of the gift of our bodies.

Steps to Reducing Stress

After Scott and Marsha realize the stress they are under and how it is hurting them, they need to take the essential steps toward reducing the stress.

This couple has several strategies available to them. All of these fall into two broad categories.

1. Things they can change
2. Things they cannot change

By the help of the Spirit, they need to live what has become known as the Serenity Prayer.

"God grant me the serenity to accept the things I cannot change, the courage to change the things I can, and the wisdom to know the difference."

Using the following model, Scott and Marsha worked out these strategies for dealing with their stress.

A Strategy for Scott

AREA	CANNOT CHANGE (So Accept)	CAN CHANGE (So Change)
Physical	Basic body type Age	Exercise Caffeine intake Proper diet—kinds and amount of food
Psychological	God-given personality Innate gifts, abilities	Dwell on positive concerning: boss situation coworkers
Behavioral	Boss's behavior	Improve job performance Learn from job review Seek to be caring and cooperative Be assertive but not confrontational Modify sleep/rest habits
Environmental	Company culture Company merger	Make minor changes in personal work space, to enhance privacy Request transfer Explore other job possibilities
Spiritual	God's unfailing, unconditional love God's presence	Daily time with the Lord, meditating on His Word, allowing it to shape thinking Serve God through job, working as for the Lord

After completing Scott's chart, they worked on Marsha's. It included most of the same elements as Scott's but with the following differences.

A Strategy for Marsha

AREA	CANNOT CHANGE (So Accept)	CAN CHANGE (So Change)
Environmental		Ask for more responsibility
		Take one college course
		Attend a relevant seminar
		Enlist help of family in household duties
		Develop efficiency plan and share it with boss

Although this was Scott's and Marsha's first effort at improving their stress management, they were well on their way. They decided to set aside a little time each Saturday morning to share spiritual discoveries from their own daily times with the Lord, to pray, and to plan together.

Six months after implementing this strategy

- their blood pressure was lower
- Scott was less irritable
- Marsha not only had regained her enthusiasm but also had finished her first course at the college
- their overall health had improved, and they were more relaxed
- the family was sharing more in the household chores

What about you? What is your stress level these days? And what are you able to do about it?

BACKGROUND SCRIPTURE: *Genesis 1:27-30; 2:15; 3:17-19; Proverbs 31:10-31; Ecclesiastes 2:17-24*

Randy Michael is an ordained Nazarene elder who has a doctorate in ministry and who does private counseling and serves as a consultant to businesses, training managers how to improve their skills in dealing with people. He and his family live in Olathe, Kans.

5

When It Seems
You're Not a Success

"Work Hard, Do Better"
Has Even Invaded the Church

by Randall Davey

I DON'T THINK I ever heard my grandfather utter the word *success*, much less discuss it. As far as I know, he never experienced stress at having not achieved it.

Grandpa lived some 87 years on the wooded, 37-acre farm where he was born. Though it was not choice Ohio farmland, he and his wife managed to raise crops, cattle, and three children.

His name was Casey Frame. He was a simple man in many respects. He had an eighth grade education. But he was an avid reader and had a good grasp of current affairs.

His home was of little value. It consisted of a four-room building with an enclosed porch that attached it to an old smokehouse. Only in the later years of his life did they have running water. His furniture was antique before antique was in vogue.

He didn't put much stock in cars, either. When he died, the car he had driven for nearly 40 years was as close as he got to modern transportation.

His clothes were an embarrassment to the family. Gifts of bib overalls or flannel shirts went unopened. He preferred the well-worn stuff you'd expect to see on street people.

Financially, he was really out of touch with the Wall Street crowd. According to government standards, he lived below the poverty level. He never knew that. He gave generously to Billy Graham, Rex Humbard, his country Methodist church, and practically anyone else who mailed him a letter asking for help.

Though he was a giant to me, he lived a rather obscure life. He was known and liked by neighbors and townsfolk in Lore City. But well-known he wasn't.

Was he a success? Though I would argue that he was, I have to admit that by the standards society applies, he was not.

Though my grandparents usually seemed content with their relatively humble status, more than once I remember them encouraging me to get an education. Coupled with that would be a warning not to even think about farming. "It's nothing but dirty old hard work," Grandma would say.

So it was that subtle. Do something to improve your lot in life. Get a good job. Make money. Don't do life like we have done it. They didn't say it that way, but I believe they meant it that way. They were simply singing the same song my folks, teachers, and friends were singing. Do what you can to get ahead in life.

Back in the '60s, when I was growing into a young man, "doing better" and getting a college education were synonymous. Folks said, "It doesn't matter what you study in school. If you have a degree, you will be hired over the guy or gal who doesn't have one." And they really thought that; and for a while, it seemed to be true. To prove their point, they would cite examples of people who went to school and were doing better.

Now when they were talking about "doing better," they were not referring to a state of mind. They were referring to the ability to buy new homes, cars, clothes, and stuff of that sort. I'm tempted to agree. More than once when I've heard of a peer who has just returned from a European trip, I've said, "They must be doing well" instead of speculating, "They must in debt up to their ears."

Success Mentality in the Church

Church folk don't seem to be exempt from the "work hard and do better" mentality. It's implicit in the way we talk. We're more likely to explain our improved lot in terms of "blessing" language. But we still tend to use the same standards the world does in assessing who is doing OK and who isn't. Success is measured by acquisition or achievements we can assess.

It figures, then, that many preacher types think along similar lines. The size of the church one pastors signals to some extent how he is doing in ministry. A call to a larger congregation is frequently perceived as a promotion or reward for a "job well done." Likewise, if one accepts a call to a smaller church, it's not unusual to hear someone speculate on why the pastor had to "take a step down."

I think most of the advice I received on this score was given with good intentions and my best interest at heart. It wasn't so much success language as it was progress language, and I didn't give it much thought. It was simply an unexamined assumption that influenced my thinking.

With that kind of mental programming, I stepped into the natural chain of progression: associate pastor, pastor of a home mission church, and then pastor of an established church. I reckoned with the fact that one does not get wealthy in ministry—but it certainly has other dividends. I experienced stress from time to time, like thousands of other parents, over how to finance college education for three kids while at the same time trying to plan for my own retirement. But I haven't lost a lot of sleep over what I can't afford to buy, the brand of clothing I wear, or the newness or oldness of the car I drive.

I did give some thought to "prudent" investments. And I've lost money in nearly every category possible. I bought a calf to get a taste of ranching. The calf escaped, only to be found sometime later in a poor condition; it was sold at a loss. I tried a hand at buying and selling guns but fared better at buying than selling. And then there was the lake lot. . . .

After a series of spoiled ventures, I simply accepted the fact that I would never be able to parlay a meager investment into a significant nest egg. But I would survive. And that was that, or so I thought. I had even given witness to feeling OK about the uncertainty of the future, including college for my kids and retirement for my wife and me.

When Good Health Took a Hike

Well, my philosophy worked as long as it wasn't tested. On the eve of my 39th year, I developed a mild pain in my left leg, starting at the hip and moving south. I didn't pay much attention to it, but in a matter of three days, I awakened, stepped out of bed, and fell down. My left leg wouldn't budge, and the pain was an attention grabber.

I consulted a medical journal we had around the house, concluded that I had pinched a nerve, confined myself to bed, and anticipated quick recovery. By nightfall, I recognized that I needed medical attention, crawled to the car, and offed it to the emergency room.

A few shots and $100 later, I was back home with an appointment in hand to see an orthopedic doctor. One office visit later, I was hospitalized and put on an IV drip of self-administered morphine. Within a few hours, I didn't care about the leg pain, the leg, the hospital, or the world. Four days and a series of out-of-mind experiences later, I was taken off morphine and sent to physical therapy. But it proved to be much ado for nothing. After nine days, the pain was still severe, and I still couldn't walk. Ruptured disk they said.

The operation was my first experience of that sort, save an outpatient tonsillectomy. The doc was good and the procedure went well, but I didn't. The first few days were awful, and I was an equally awful patient. My left foot felt like it was in scalding water, and I couldn't stand to have anyone touch it.

I was dismissed with the assurance that things would probably clear up pretty soon. They didn't. The burning continued and I couldn't sleep, night after night. The pain was such that I couldn't read the newspaper or even follow the plot line on reruns of the "Andy Griffith Show." I felt absolutely worthless, and to say that I was despondent and stressed was an understatement.

After a few weeks of near daily conversation with the surgeon, he suggested that I might be as good as I was going to get. I'm not a rocket scientist, but I reasoned real quickly that if I was as good as I was going to get, I wouldn't be able to do my job. I still couldn't concentrate or sleep for more than an hour at a time.

Out of curiosity, I called the district church office and inquired about the disability policy for which I was qualified. The news was devastating, and my stress level (and blood pressure) skyrocketed.

While I was still in despair over the possibility of never working again, I went back to the surgeon for additional X rays. I couldn't believe it when he said, "There's something else in there that shouldn't be. I don't know what it is, but it has to come out."

He was quite candid with me. He openly wondered if it was a tumor, but confessed he didn't know. He sent the X rays away for a second opinion, and the consulting doc agreed that whatever it was, it had to come out.

The night before the second operation was one of the longest nights of my life. I couldn't get the idea of a tumor out of my mind, and I assumed the worst. Sometime after midnight, I was overwhelmed with the impression that I would not survive the surgery; that thought never left me until I was put to sleep.

I wasn't prepared for the emotional collage of the ensuing hours. It wasn't the thought of dying that upset me so much as the thought of what I would leave behind. I thought of my wife and my kids, my extended family, and the church. At that point, I was filled with remorse because of the many loose ends with which someone else would have to deal.

It was the review of my estate that caused the problem. I thought about the stuff that I had around the house and the stuff that I couldn't pay for if I was on disability. And now that I might possibly die, it would be an absolutely awful mess for my wife to handle.

My mind was alive with pictures. It was as though someone had taken a camcorder and had gone from room to room and from year to year, capturing all the dumb things I had ever said, done, and bought.

The lake lot came to mind. The partially restored '51 Chevy in the garage. The seldom-used (and never used well) golf clubs in my closet. The touring bike hanging from a rafter in the garage. Stuff upon stuff. I was anxious because I knew I couldn't possibly do anything about anything. Only a few hours left till surgery, and then . . .

I was haunted. Haunted by the stressful conversations my wife and I had about college, braces, and retirement, none of which would be a concern to a corpse. The big deals of my life—church attendance, members in, members out—seemed laughable. I simply could not look at my performance of the first 39 years and say, "Well done." And now, there was no time left. Family and friends arrived about 6 A.M., and I wept quietly as I said what I was sure would be my final good-bye.

No tumor. It was one of those "We've never had a case like yours before" scenarios, but no tumor. Long recovery. Three months out of the pulpit, and vivid memories of the night that was.

It Changed My Outlook on Life

All this was a life-altering experience, to say the least. In the months of recovery at home, I pledged to myself that I would "travel more lightly," ridding myself of stuff that I didn't need. I gave the golf clubs away, the bike, the '51 Chevy, the lake lot, and I put a "For Sale" sign on a few other things. A lot of stress went too.

It's been a year since that ordeal started, and it's been a good year of evaluation. I've had opportunity to think about the kinds of things I've said to my kids about what matters, and I've wondered to what extent I have sent them confusing and fraudulent messages.

"What are you going to be when you get big?" I've asked. An innocent question but maybe a very unimportant one. Maybe I should say to my kids, "Whatever you choose to do, do it to the glory of God." I was well into my adult years before I understood that the chief end of humanity is to glorify God.

I wonder what messages I've sent concerning money. I wonder if I have communicated the value in using money to advance the Kingdom, or will my kids simply conclude that vocation is about getting a big pile of stuff.

The problem, then, is not with one's desire to be successful but the standards by which success is measured. If the standard is money, prestige, or power, one will probably live in perpetual stress, striving for more of each. If one understands success in Kingdom terms, the categories of measurement are drastically different.

The more I think about it, the more I believe that my grandfather was a successful man. He'll not be listed among the Trumps, Rockefellers, or Iaccocas, but he was a success.

He was successful in saying to his family that what God has to say matters. He worshiped. On the tractor, in the fields, in the barn, and in the church, he worshiped. He talked frequently about the Lord, and spiritual issues were a dominant part of his conversations. He really did glorify the Lord.

He was successful in saying to his children and grandchildren that fulfillment can be found in laying down your life for others. Clearly, it wasn't about increasing your assets, for he used what he had to advance the Kingdom, or at least that was his intention.

He was successful in saying, "Nevertheless it's not I who live in Christ, but Christ who lives in me" (see Galatians 2:20, KJV). He said it to me. He said it to his friends. And he said it without saying it.

My dreams are different these days.

I dream that the church can really become a community of people committed to the worship of God, given to studying His Word, open to serving Him and humankind, eager to give witness to His coming again. A community of people where acceptance is not based on status, wealth, color, or race. A community of people who model for a stress-laden world what it means to delight in God and live for Him. I want my family to be part of that kind of community where success is understood in light of the person and ministry of Jesus Christ.

And that's my ongoing prayer for us all. "Thy kingdom come. Thy will be done in earth, as it is in heaven" (Matthew 6:10, KJV).

BACKGROUND SCRIPTURE: John 15:5-14; Colossians 3:1-3, 17

Randall Davey is senior pastor of the Overland Park Church of the Nazarene, Overland Park, Kans.

6

When Woe Are Your Finances

Money Fights
Don't Have to Tear
Your Family Apart

by Richard A. Fish

YOU DON'T HAVE TO BE POOR to get upset and stressed about money.

I have counseled widows on low fixed incomes who are more at peace about their finances than millionaires are.

Not only does stress over money affect people at all levels of income, it intrudes into the entire life of those it affects. That's because finances and possessions influence so many areas of a person's life: self-concept, relationships, sense of security, hope for the future.

The good news is that with a healthy attitude, a little financial knowledge, and a bit of discipline, anyone can learn to reduce their stress over money.

But before you can reduce the stress, you have to recognize you have it.

Here are a few symptoms.

- feeling that you'll never get out of debt
- worrying about how you're going to pay the bills
- arguing with family members about money
- sensing inferiority feelings about your job, clothing, or home
- having strong emotional responses to news about the economy or the stock market
- believing that forces beyond your control are determining your life-style or financial security

Money, a Sign of God's Favor?

Jesus' disciples lived in a Jewish culture that believed wealth was a sign of God's favor. That is why the Twelve were so amazed when Jesus told them it was especially hard for rich people to make it into the Kingdom (Matthew 19:23-25).

Even today, in the church, wealthy Christians often get more power and respect. Speakers or musicians who charge the highest fee are often considered the best. (Why else would they charge so much?) Money and possessions may become a way of "keeping score" of how successful a person is.

One Christian couple I know has continually upgraded their house, car, and other possessions because they are concerned about their image. I'll call them Emily and Bill. They are living a life-style far beyond either of their parents. In their 20 years of marriage they have traded houses three times, each time moving into a more expensive one. They presently live in a four-bedroom house in a nice neighborhood. But the last I heard, Emily had her eye on a six-bedroom antique with five working fireplaces. And Bill was thinking about buying an expensive foreign car.

These new purchases will require them to trade more time for money. And it will increase their stress. But it will also make them stand out more in their church and community.

Given our society's tendency to measure a person's worth by adding up their income and possessions, it's not easy for Christians to do otherwise. It takes personal and spiritual maturity. But the rewards are a reduction in stress and the ability to experience joy in the success of others.

This is an area, however, in which we need to respect individual differences. Your teenagers and spouse may feel the need to spend more money than you do because of self-esteem issues or past deprivations.

Another source of money-related stress comes from worrying about the things you own. This, too, can stem from self-esteem issues. Our sense of self-worth can become attached to the possessions, or "trophies," we've earned. So, these things become extensions of ourselves.

The first scratch on the new car can be a source of dread and unkind words toward a spouse. "You let the guy back into you? Why do you think they invented the horn?"

The antique chair in the living room can become protected at the expense of a guest's feelings. "I'm sorry, you can't sit in that chair. It's 150 years old."

One way to test your attitude toward your possessions is to imagine returning home from a day at work. As you turn the corner onto your street, you see your house has burned to the ground. How much do you think this would affect your life?

If you think the lost possessions would leave you with the lingering feeling that your life has been ruined, you're probably carrying around too much money-related stress. But if knowing that people and pets are safe is what is most important, you have eliminated a big source of stress.

When we acknowledge the Lord's ownership of the things in our possession, we hold them more loosely. And we share them more willingly.

Family Arguments over Money

A common source of stress and conflict for married couples stems from the different ways their families handled money and possessions. The husband might come from a family that lived on the edge of their credit limits. And the wife might come from a family that never, ever, bought on credit. They saved for years so they could pay cash for a car.

I advise couples to write a financial autobiography describing how their families dealt with finances. A wife who was raised in a situation where parents saved before buying will certainly be at odds with a husband who learned to borrow and take risks to get ahead. Discussing these differences can be a basis for working out a compromise.

This isn't the only reason couples argue about money. Sometimes unrelated issues, such as sharing decision-making power, get played out in conflicts over finances. A wife who feels dominated by her husband may spend money irresponsibly as a way to steal some power or get back at her spouse. Couples need to talk about their differences so that they can make the necessary changes in their behavior. Counseling is often helpful when people find themselves stuck in long-standing destructive patterns of relating to others.

Some of the most intense financial stress can come from transactions between friends and family members. Because of this, I advise that the terms for buying and selling property and lending money should always be put in writing and honored. It is fine to give a friend or family member a special deal. But making the agreements perfectly clear may avoid future conflict and stress.

Mental Health Money

A lot of people live from paycheck to paycheck. They set aside no money for savings. This can be the source of long-term stress and hopelessness. A minor car repair or dental bill can blow the tight budget. And becoming unemployed for even a short time can be devastating.

I advise every family or single individual to save 10 percent of their income as "mental health money." This fund can be kept in long-term deposit programs of banks or in government bonds. This should never be touched, no matter how tight the budget. In addition, I recommend an emergency fund you can tap into for unexpected expenses. This second savings program should be kept separate from the "mental health money." In difficult times, knowing you are not completely broke can be a source of stress relief.

Having a decent place to live and enough money to pay living expenses is so basic to a sense of well-being that purchasing a home should usually be the next investment project after the "mental health fund" and emergency fund. Lack of control over rent increases, home maintenance, and even eviction can be a cause of ongoing stress.

Plan Your Spending

To save money, buy a home, and invest for retirement, a family needs to have a spending plan or budget. Stress can often be increased by the unknown. Not knowing how much money is coming in, where it has gone, or how much you owe is bound to be stressful.

Every budget plan should include a personal allowance for each family member. One dollar per week for each year of age is one simple method to determine the amount —if you can afford that much. Having a certain amount of money under your control for personal expenses can be uplifting for a person of any age. There is something demeaning to be an adult or a child who has to beg a parent figure for a dollar to buy a treat.

Being in debt can become a source of great stress. Borrowing to purchase a home is usually a wise investment, as long as payments fit the budget. But credit card debt for goods consumed immediately, such as food, is one of the worst investments if the balance cannot be paid in full each month.

Spending more than present income is spending future income. After reviewing the telephone bill once, I informed our 13-year-old daughter she had spent her allowance through age 18. Many adults get into serious financial trouble living beyond their current income.

One way to avoid going beyond your budget with credit card purchases is to subtract the charges from the checkbook balance as they occur. If you keep a positive balance, the money should be there to pay the bills in full each month.

Some stressful debt and unwise spending is the result of unplanned and compulsive spending. One way to avoid impulse buying is described in Richard Foster's book *Freedom of Simplicity*. He suggests we wait to buy something expensive we think we need. First, he suggests we wait to see if it comes to us without our having to buy it. If after two weeks we haven't received it, we can reconsider the purchase and buy it if we think we still need it. I have saved a great deal of money this way and have had wonderful experiences giving and receiving.

If you are unable to pay current bills because of lowered income, an emergency, or overwhelming debt, don't ignore the situation. Contact creditors, tell them the situation, and try to agree on modified payment plans. Sometimes it is necessary to seek the help of a nonprofit counseling service that will help negotiate with your creditors.

Because people are living longer after retirement, it is more important than ever to invest some of our present income to avoid financial stress in the future. Those with considerable extra income should live simply so that they can save more and provide for the needs of others in retirement and not just for themselves.

Don't Overdo the Insurance

Adequate insurance for financial risks can provide some important peace of mind. Only buy the insurance you really need, and shop for the best deals.

Good health insurance, for example, is a necessity for everyone. But some people use their limited insurance dollars unwisely. As a result, they increase their stress rather than reduce it.

A couple I'll call Matt and Jennifer came to me for help because they were under extreme financial pressures over large car payments. In looking at their agreement from the dealer, I discovered they had been sold life insurance and mechanical breakdown insurance at outrageously high prices. In addition, they were paying a high rate of interest to borrow money for the coverage.

When they learned more about the insurance and questioned the dealer, they made a more informed choice. They lowered the payments and decreased their stress.

Using God's Resources

Most people waste precious financial resources because of a lack of knowledge. They simply don't make the effort to be good stewards. Because all our money and possessions belong to the Lord, learning how to handle finances is an obligation of every Christian.

We are not only to care for our own families, but also to manage the storehouses of assets to carry on God's work and to care for others. It is an exciting and awesome responsibility.

There are many ways we can lessen the stress of others by using the resources God has put in our care.

We can support the ministry of our church by tithing. We can lend money at good rates and terms. We can sell at below market prices. We can treat people to meals or to a weekend getaway trip.

Other important services involve time rather than money. We can baby-sit small children so that a young couple can have an evening out together. We can help an elderly person with a tax return. Or we can simply be available to listen and give emotional support.

Holidays and anniversaries can be a costly and stressful time for some people because of the expectation of giving. If in gift giving it is the thought that counts, you can send as good a thought with $5.00 as with $500. For the past 10 years my wife and I have escaped the stress of Christmas gift giving by setting a low limit ($5.00-$15.00) for gifts for each other. We give more money away to the truly needy than we spend on our family. It has been wonderfully relaxing to shop at the last minute for gifts when you have only $10.00 to spend.

Some stress comes from greed. A person who has enough money to live comfortably yet who continues to trade time and energy for an ever higher life-style or who tries always to come out way ahead on each transaction is headed for unnecessary stress (Luke 12:15-21). This hunger for more may come from a sense of inferiority, from irrational insecurity, or from buying into the secular world's idea of how to measure success. When checking stock and bond prices in the daily newspaper becomes a regular source of stress, something is wrong.

The key to reducing financial stress is to learn to live out the truth that all we are and have belongs to the Lord. As God's stewards, we have the responsibility to learn as much as we can about effectively managing these financial resources and putting the knowledge to work.

We need to get away from measuring personal worth in financial terms. And we need to develop a sense of community where we help each other live at a reasonable level. The Early Church seemed to be on the right track. "The whole group of those who believed were of one heart and soul, and no one claimed private ownership of any possessions . . . With great power the apostles gave testimony to the resurrection of the Lord Jesus, and great grace was upon them all. There was not a needy person among them" (Acts 4:32-34, NRSV).

Living in a sense of community, we should be willing to let our personal and financial needs be known. And we should be ready to both give and accept help.

BACKGROUND SCRIPTURE: Matthew 19:23-25; Luke 12:15-21; Acts 4:32-35

Richard A. Fish is a psychology professor at Eastern Nazarene College, Quincy, Mass. He coordinates the master's program in family counseling and teaches courses on financial counseling in family therapy.

7

They're Christians, but I Want to Wring Their Necks

Some Saints Squabble over Shrubbery, Coffee, and the Pastor's Shoes

by Leola Floren Gee

THE CHURCH is white frame, tiny, and occupied on Sundays and Wednesday nights by a congregation that knows by heart "We're Marching to Zion" and "What a Friend We Have in Jesus." Most of the folks don't need a hymnal unless the song leader calls for the third verse. And he knows better than to rock the boat by doing that.

A friend of mine attends there. I'll call him Bill. He and his wife have two daughters. One daughter plays the piano, and the other plays the organ. Bill leads the singing, makes the announcements, teaches a Sunday School class, welcomes everyone at the door, and makes sure the visiting minister has a place to eat lunch.

The congregation—teachers, small business owners, homemakers, retired people—scraped together enough money for the walls and roof of the church when they built it, but they didn't have any left over for landscaping. So for a decade the building lay with the dust from the fields drifting up against the wooden steps.

Bill was a member of the board, so at a meeting he suggested that shrubbery—perhaps some little pines— might improve the looks of the place and lift the spirits of the congregation.

Most everyone agreed it was a good idea, but there was a problem: Once the pines were planted, who would water them? Without proper care they would shrivel up and die, and who would be willing to take on the responsibility?

Better not, the board decided. With no guarantee that anyone would water the pines, they'd better skip it. Bill and his family were disappointed, and the church building remained something of an eyesore in the community.

The Church Divided

Is it silly for the saints to squabble over shrubbery? Sure. Is it uncommon? Not at all.

It seems ironic that something so innocuous as a few pine trees could drive a wedge between church members, but issues big and small have divided and disrupted the Body of Christ for as long as the Church has been around.

Today, Christians debate how to handle the problem of sexual immorality in the church. Two thousand years ago, they were doing the same thing.

Today, Christians can't agree over church leadership. Two thousand years ago, the apostle Paul wrote on the same subject.

Today, congregations complain sermons are too long. Two thousand years ago, a church member went to sleep and fell out of a window (Acts 20:9).

The gift of the Holy Spirit, the role of women, how finances should be managed—each of these issues re-surfaces in some fashion, in every generation, and still we haven't figured out how to work through our differences and get along. Ever wonder what those two churchwomen Euodia and Syntyche were squabbling about in Philippians 4:2? Perhaps one of them wanted to plan an elaborate menu for the church social, and the other wanted potluck.

While it should go without saying that Christians should never compromise on ethical matters that are clearly spelled out in Scripture, many of our differences have to do with personal taste, style, upbringing, and cul-ture.

In fact, the issues that cause broken relationships and hurt feelings—and sometimes split congregations—often have little or nothing to do with matters of theological ac-curacy. Instead, they have to do with music, landscaping, and the color of the new carpeting or choir robes.

As I prepared to write this chapter, I called Dr. Norman Shawchuck. He's director of Spiritual Growth Resources in Chicago and a consultant for religious organizations on conflict management. He has helped many congregations sort out their differences. He has this to say about the source of stress within the church: "There are thousands of [causes]. A group doesn't like the way the preacher preaches a sermon, or a group is bent out of shape because the church hired a youth minister. Churches have come nearly to the point of splitting because they didn't like the pastor not having his shoes shined."

Minor issues don't get settled, and before you know it they've turned into major issues, and people are lined up on opposite sides looking for ammunition. Sadly enough, "Just about all conflicts grow out of misunderstanding," says Shawchuck. "It's a function of poor communication."

Case in point: A man at the church I attend glared at me one Sunday morning because he caught me taking a cup of coffee from the table just outside his class. If I could have pried open his brain at that moment and read the unspoken comments, I imagine they would have gone something like this: "I can't believe the nerve of some people! Why doesn't she get coffee in her own class? We pay for all this stuff, and here she is helping herself."

He had no idea, of course, that I routinely slipped a dollar into the cup marked "Coffee Fund" to cover my habit. I figure my contributions more than covered the cost of the Sanka packets I consumed while teaching a group of high schoolers in a room down the hall.

At that point I should have explained my situation, and asked his permission to continue, or offered to seek my morning cup of coffee elsewhere.

I'm sorry to say I did no such thing. I smiled, took my coffee, and thought to myself, What a grouch. There must be better ways of handling a misunderstanding.

Steps Toward Reconciliation

Whatever the cause of the conflict—ranging from a pilfered cup of coffee to disagreement over whether to replace the KJVs in the pews with NIVs—someone needs to take the first step toward resolving the matter. That's the advice of Shawchuck, author of *How to Manage Conflict in the Church.*

First, someone has to start a conversation about the situation. It should include all the persons who are involved in the conflict or misunderstanding.

If everyone can get together in a friendly and relaxed setting and talk things through, great. However, it may be necessary, if the conflict is very serious, for a person with good communication skills to help by gathering everyone's impressions and opinions, and repeating them to the assembled group. This helps clarify statements and gives everyone an opportunity to explain his viewpoint and better understand what the conflict is really about.

In addition, that person can help both sides see areas in which they agree. "We can come to think pretty quickly that we disagree on everything, and in general, that's not true," says Shawchuck.

It's important to remember that as long as communication lines remain open, an area of conflict or stress can be turned into a creative problem-solving session in which disagreeing individuals can work together to find a solution with which both are content. This negotiation stage may not always flow smoothly and may require compromise on both sides.

Ironically, it's because we are a church "family" that it's so easy for us to be hurt by one another during this process.

"It's not a perfect world," says Shawchuck. "No relationship is tension free. When we are experiencing these things with people we love a lot, our emotions get mixed up; I can be far more patient with the guy who puts gas in my car than with my wife; the closer the relationship, the higher the expectations."

And so it's quite understandable that the church, filled with imperfect people whose quest is ultimate perfection, find themselves at odds with one another. To further complicate matters, as evangelicals who believe we are led by the Holy Spirit, it's easy for us to believe our opinions and plans have the divine seal of approval.

As Shawchuck puts it, "If the Word is infallible, and I am the bearer of the Word, it's an easy step for me to say MY word is infallible." Pastors can fall into that trap, but don't be too hard on them—the rest of us can fall into the trap too.

When You're Rejected

What if you want to make peace, and the enemy—who happens to be your brother or sister in Christ—is still stockpiling warheads? You want to negotiate a settlement, but the other party has no interest in restoring the relationship.

According to Shawchuck, "Someone with integrity and fortitude needs to say, 'You have to get together, and you WILL get together.'" Very often this will be the role of the pastor or a highly respected lay leader.

If people absolutely refuse to come together, the question must be asked: Should the church leadership allow this conflict to continue to pull apart the congregation? Or should the church board or other leaders say, "Look, you can't go on with this, or the consequences could be very grave"? If the feuding parties resist efforts at reconciliation, the congregation or board should decide the outcome. But this rarely happens, according to Shawchuck.

Nevertheless, he says, "Removing people from the fellowship can be done amiably; that's not the biggest danger. The biggest danger is allowing people to go on fighting and tearing up the congregation."

It is critical that the situation be dealt with and not allowed to fester, because unresolved anger has devastating consequences. Lewis B. Smedes, author of *Forgive and Forget: Healing the Hurts We Don't Deserve*, identifies specific stages in what he calls the miracle of forgiveness. The offended party progresses from hurt, to hatred, to healing, and—in some cases—reconciliation with the one responsible for the hurt. Forgiveness is by no means automatic or effortless, and Shawchuck warns that some choose to live with malice instead.

It's easy to say that for Christians forgiveness is essential, but what if the offense is so great or traumatic, and so blatantly contrary to scriptural principles, that reconciliation would seem to be unlikely? For example, what if a member of the board is found to have committed adultery with a member of the church staff, and both are unrepentant? Then, says Shawchuck, the goal is to "bring people to charity and understanding and forgiveness, rather than to allow that relationship to be severed with sins of hatred and unresolved anger that will haunt the congregation for years."

In other words, people need to talk to each other with the intention of identifying the causes of stress and division, and take the necessary steps to either deal with the sin (if sin is involved), or compromise on their preferences.

Lighten Up

Dr. James Mullins, pastor of Heights First Church of the Nazarene in Albuquerque, N.Mex., tells the story of a monk who asks a dour pilgrim if he knows why angels fly.

The pilgrim, who has far more serious things on his mind, considers it a ridiculous question.

Patiently, the monk answers his own question: "Angels can fly, because they take themselves so lightly."

As Pastor Mullins points out, we Christians should take God seriously and ourselves more lightly.

That's what Bill, the song leader at the little white church did. Remember those pine trees? He quietly broached the subject again, and he met with the same response from the church board, "But who will water the pines?"

This time Bill was ready with an answer. "I will."

Within a few days they were in place, scrubby shoots that looked like rejects from a Christmas tree farm. In time they branched out and grew thicker stems, and by late summer they formed a crisp green collar around the building's foundation.

Somewhere along the line, "But who will water the pines?" turned into a family joke at Bill's house, a quick squelch to anybody's outrageous and fanciful suggestion: "Let's sell the car, take the money, and spend a wild weekend at Disneyland!"

"Good idea," someone would counter, "but we can't. Who will water the pines?"

The pines were taken care of, and one small corner of the Kingdom is more pleasant for their presence. Perhaps even more important, a source of irritation and division was transformed into a source of good-natured laughter.

It doesn't take a doctorate in psychology to spot the type of person who wants to plant pines, and the type who will think of a hundred excellent reasons why pines shouldn't be planted. Our churches are filled with both, and there's room for both.

What there isn't room for is fighting about it.

BACKGROUND SCRIPTURE: *Genesis 13:4-9; Matthew 18:15-17; I Corinthians 1:10-13; Galatians 2:11-14*

Leola Floren Gee is a free-lance writer, a member of the Church of the Nazarene, and a newspaper columnist in Novi, Mich.

8

Time-Crunched at the Church

There Is Such a Thing
as Too Many Meetings

by Mark R. Littleton

WHEN I WROTE an article on the time crunch for *Moody Monthly,* a reader responded with a letter to the editor. He wrote, "Littleton paints the church as a victim of life's pressures. The Bible and experience picture it as a refuge.

"The church, not the world, should be the pacesetter by keeping its Sunday evening and Wednesday services alive and well attended through Spirit-filled ministry."[1]

I agree with the man who wrote this. The church shouldn't be a victim of life's pressures. It should be "the pacesetter." Above all it should feature "well-attended ... services" that are characterized by "Spirit-filled ministry."

But what if it isn't a pacesetter?

What if the services aren't characterized by "Spirit-filled ministry," but by

- poorly prepared sermons
- poorly executed music and specials
- 20 percent of the people doing all the work, and the rest just looking on
- a general lack of enthusiasm about anything spiritual

- a pastor working 70-80 hours a week with no end in sight?

If that's your church, it's bound to make people feel confused, angry, and unwilling to give their time and effort to the ministry.

Our Lukewarm Church

I don't mean to condemn the modern church or to say all churches come under the above description. Clearly, there are many strong, Spirit-filled leaders and churches out there.

It's just that, well, frankly, they seem so few and far between.

I honestly think much of the church in our nation today finds its sister in the Laodicean church of Revelation 3:14-22. Look at verses 15-17: "I know your deeds, that you are neither cold nor hot. I wish you were either one or the other! So, because you are lukewarm—neither hot nor cold—I am about to spit you out of my mouth. You say, 'I am rich; I have acquired wealth and do not need a thing.' But you do not realize that you are wretched, pitiful, poor, blind and naked."

Dr. Michael Green, associate professor of field education at Dallas Theological Seminary, comments on the low attendance we see in many churches: "Sunday evening in many churches is dead. Wednesday night prayer meeting is a ghost. It's impossible to maintain these programs in many churches."

Notice the emphasis, though, on "many." Not all. Not even most. But does that mean we should shut down services?

Not necessarily. Simply cutting back because the services aren't packed out doesn't mean the "faithful few" shouldn't be nourished.

What is clear is that only quality programs and ministries will attract the average saint. If the worshiper doesn't get anything out of it, why put anything into it? Granted, the "What's in it for me?" outlook is selfish. But if we can't get people to listen to the message, how can we teach them the truth of their own need for God?

Too often, though, "the church seems to be the last one to figure out what's going on," adds Tim Kimmel, author of *Little House on the Freeway*, and president of Generation Ministries. "The whole system punishes the traditional family. The school system abuses them. The government offers them no tax breaks. And the church takes advantage of the 'nice' folks who can't seem to say no. Then they burn out."

Disappearing Volunteers

Women used to be a mainstay of the church's structure. They had the time and could volunteer to help out where the men couldn't. No more. Dr. Green says, "They were available to provide unbudgeted labor. Now the church not only has to hire a youth pastor and a minister of Christian education, but someone to do the women's ministries, the children's ministries. It's becoming more profession—less of a servant atmosphere."

Ramona Tucker, an editor with Harold Shaw Publishers, has worked with teens for nearly 6 years; her husband has been involved for 10. They have recently pulled out for personal reasons. She commented, "One problem is that many wives' husbands don't even come to church. That's one pressure. Then the younger wives with small children only want to work with groups that have their children. After that you have older women who feel they gave their part in their younger years, and now the young women should be doing the main work. It's getting so churches simply have to hire people to do everything."

But the cry for something to "meet my needs" has even hit the very heart of the ministry, the pastor's home. A pastor's wife said, "I'm involved in a Bible study at *another* church. I was leading one in my husband's church, but it wasn't fulfilling. I wanted people to get to know the Lord better. But the group wanted to go in another direction. So I found a group in another church that desired that." If pastor's wives are bailing out, what hope is there for the rest of us?

Clearly, fewer women are able to devote the time and effort they once had.

Skipping Church

Another area that has affected the church dramatically is the radical social changes of the past few years. There are more working mothers, single parents, stepfamilies, and people with nontraditional sexual orientations than ever before. All this has affected the family's role in the church.

The result is that some Christians are actually taking refuge from the church. They're refusing to go to all the meetings in favor of having a fairly normal family life at home.

What people lament even more is the decline they see in many churches. An article in *Time* reported, "The central fact about mainline Protestantism in the U.S. today is that it is in deep trouble. The stunning turnabout is apparent in the unprecedented hemorrhaging of memberships in the three major faiths that date from colonial times."[2]

Those three major denominations are the United Church of Christ, down 20 percent since 1965; the Presbyterian church, down 25 percent; and the Episcopal church, down 28 percent.

What's the Problem?

So what is the problem that people are experiencing?

"The main reason I've never joined a church is simply because I knew I couldn't give it the time I should," says Carey Price, a furniture sales manager in a Sears store in Hunt Valley, Md. "Really giving yourself takes a lot of time," he said. "And I just don't have it with the other ministries I'm involved in."

Carey is involved heavily in working with a Christian camp and is a leader in CBMC (Christian Businessmen's Committee), a businessmen's organization that seeks to make disciples in the context of one's daily work. For personal reasons he sees these as the significant uses of his time over service in his church.

Another businessman, Dave Buettell, a sales engineer with Reliance Electric in Baltimore, told me, "Frankly, when is enough enough? You get pressure from people in the church. You feel a responsibility to your family. But mostly you just feel guilty. You feel you can't say no. It's an incredible tension."

Randy Schiller, another businessman, summed it all up this way: "I never used to have this problem until I became a member of a church."

Meetinged Out

Jesus did discipleship. The modern church talks about it. Jesus had a ministry. The modern church, unfortunately, seems to be an endless stream of meetings.

Dr. Joseph Werner, a podiatrist in Cockeysville, Md., runs four offices and has three other partners. He's on the board of directors of two Christian schools, is heavily involved in CBMC like Carey Price, and also spends much of his weekend in the church. He says, "Our biggest problem is the inability to have a consistent family meal at home. Too often I'm out for evening meetings and have my wife and children meet me outside the home for dinner between work and meetings.

"Meetings have become a four-letter word to my children. Too often I'm not able to help with homework or their projects. Nothing is done at a leisurely pace in our home with any family member. Taking a break usually requires vacation time or at least having the phone off the hook."

With the modern church you can spend most of your life in meetings. Worship meetings. Committee meetings. Youth group meetings. Sunday School class meetings. Social gatherings. You name it. Fellowship is the reason, but meetings are the season.

One man who asked to remain anonymous said, "My dad spent a lot of time in the church. He had his own business. And either he was working late or was at church. He hardly ever did anything with me. I resented it. I still do."

As you study the New Testament, you don't get the impression there were meetings on the level and at the pace of present-day society. Most of the "meetings" you find in the Book of Acts are either spontaneous evangelistic "events" or prayer times organized in response to some special event. Much of the teaching was done house by house, or in the Temple. There simply does not appear to be the systematization you find in the church today.

The question is: have we substituted meetings for true spirituality?

Don Hawkins, executive director of the Minirth-Meier Clinic and host of the radio program by the same name, comments, "The evangelical church has fed into the hurried society by scheduling too many events—and then pressuring people into doing too much. All in the name of Christian service."

He adds that the church itself is "very reluctant to jettison programs. They feel that somehow they're displeasing God—violating Scripture—if they terminate a program or two. And the false guilt factor goes up."

Rev. Brent Brooks, a church-planting pastor in Columbia, Md., sees this as a serious problem and hindrance, not only to real spirituality and success but also to building disciples. "The multiple-meeting format and the heavily bureaucratized structure of most churches," he says, "gives them trouble getting commitment from their people. People feel stressed out. Sunday used to be a day of relaxation." But now it's hurry, hurry, hurry—from one meeting to the next.

No one is claiming the church ought to terminate all meetings, committee work, group ministries, socials, and other forms of fellowship, evangelism, and worship. But it's obvious people are reaching their limits. Considering that Sunday night services and even Wednesday prayer meetings are a modern invention, there's nothing sacred in either. God has not given us the form; He's provided the function. That is, He told us what to do; He hasn't told us in all cases, and especially in the area of meetings and services, *how* to do it.

Sacrificing Quality

Perhaps part of the problem is not just the number of meetings, but the quality of the ones we can attend. They're just not up to snuff, soul, or spirit!

When it comes to growth, many evangelical churches are in a holding pattern or in the same kind of decline as the mainline denominations.

Unfortunately, the joy and power of Christianity—which is people living out their faith in homes, workplaces, and marketplaces—has been subtly transformed. Now we meet in the church to keep the machine going rather than to be trained to go out.

The result is that people burn out or burn up. Some even rebel. What they're saying is: "Either make the meetings you have more meaningful and more worthwhile, or I won't come."

Is this plain selfishness?

To some degree—but not only on the part of the church member. Selfishness runs right through the whole spectrum, from pastors and leaders who are neither pastoring nor leading, to the lazy lamb who doesn't want to lose his TV time.

Time for a Change

There must be change. But what kind?

The complaints I have seen about the church and its many meetings may be summarized as follows:

- too many services that don't teach, inspire, or encourage real worship
- meetings that go on and on
- meetings that have no content
- too many other outside activities
- too many things I have to force my kids, my family, and myself to go to
- too little real worship and enjoyment of God

After a while, a person gets so tired of it all, he pulls back and says, "What's the use? I'll do something else." So they get involved in meaningful organizations outside the church—parachurch or otherwise.

What's the answer? Here are some suggestions I've pulled together from a questionnaire I distributed.

1. Become an expert at something.

I once heard a preacher say, "An expert is someone who knows no more than you do, but he has it better organized and uses slides."

Perhaps. But there is something to concentrating on one thing. George Washington Carver is quoted as asking God to tell him the secrets of the universe. God said that was too big; he should choose something smaller. So Carver asked to know the mysteries of the peanut. Apparently God answered that one because Carver's discoveries are still with us today.

There is tremendous satisfaction in mastering a subject or developing your skills in one facet of life. Perhaps our time crunch is because we have chosen to study the forest rather than the tree, or the leaf, or even the stem. Instead of running around to a mass of activities, try concentrating on just one.

This applies especially to families with children. We parents want the best for our kids, and rightly so. But we can all wear ourselves out by having too many places to run to, too much equipment to purchase, and too many performances to attend. Instead, pick out one or two and concentrate on doing them well.

2. Learn to do one job in the church and do it well; then add if you want.

I heard this principle repeatedly from the people who filled out my questionnaire. Only take on more jobs in the church if you have *one* under control.

Paul said, "This one thing I do." The converse to that is, "These many things I don't do!"

Similarly, 19th-century evangelist Dwight L. Moody wrote, "Give me a man who says, 'This one thing I do' like Paul, and not, 'These 50 things I dabble in.'"

Resist the dabbling syndrome. You have to choose: will

I have a quality ministry, or spread myself so thin that no one even feels its effect?

Judy Winter, a pastor's wife in Denver, told me, "In our last church, I decided not to sing in the choir. I had to prioritize, and I couldn't give it the work it deserved. I've learned that my first year in a church I only do one thing, usually join a circle. And no committees!"

Bill Tamulonis, a young businessman, said, "We limit the number of activities I and my wife are involved in to two per week. Right now we're involved in a class on marriage and our house church. We don't schedule *anything else* that meets regularly."

3. Refuse to do something just because it's there.

Many people take on jobs in the church "because if I don't do it, it won't get done." Maybe it's better to leave it undone!

Please understand, I'm not advocating a selfish outlook that says, "It doesn't coincide with my goals; therefore I'm not doing it." Rather, we need to have the same kind of servant attitude that Jesus had. Larry Dyer put it this way: "Time management insists that you force others to serve your considerations, but the Greatest Role Model said, 'The Son of Man did not come to be served, but to serve.'"

But even Jesus set His limits. When the crowd closed in around Him in Matthew 8:18, He "gave orders to cross to the other side of the lake." He had priorities, goals, and a mission to accomplish. He didn't simply do things because they were available.

4. Concentrate on today.

Newspaper columnist Sydney J. Harris said, "The art of living successfully consists of being able to hold two opposite ideas in tension at the same time: first, to make long-term plans as if we were going to live forever; and second, to conduct ourselves as if we were going to die tomorrow."

Today is all we have. We never know whether it's our last. The jack-of-all-trades has 20 tasks going on at once, perhaps with none finished. The expert concentrates on one. He not only gets something done but gets it done well and with a relaxed, happy smile on his face.

There's the old story of the farmer who went out hunting with his hound dog. When the farmer returned, he still seemed fresh, but the dog flopped down on the porch, exhausted. Someone asked him what was wrong, and he said, "Well, it wasn't the walking. We only covered 10 miles. But there wasn't a gate open along the way that he didn't go in and examine the whole field. Not a cat appeared but that he had to chase it—rabbits, too. And there wasn't a dog barked but that he wore himself out barking back and showing fight. He must have gone 50 miles to my 10. No, it weren't the route that got him, but the zig-zagging."[3]

I fear that the time crunch we feel is because of our zigzag life-styles. Instead, we must home in on the target and reach it.

1. Robert H. Surpless, letter to the editor, *Moody Monthly,* July/August, 1989, 10.
2. Richard N. Ostling, "Those Mainline Blues," *Time,* May 22, 1989, 94.
3. Quoted in *Bits and Pieces,* May 1980, 12-78.

BACKGROUND SCRIPTURE: *Acts 2:41-47; Hebrews 10:22-25; Revelation 3:14-22*

Mark R. Littleton is a full-time free-lance writer and the author of several books including *Escaping the Time Crunch* (Moody Press), from which this chapter is condensed. He lives with his wife and two children in Hunt Valley, Md.

9

Sex Problems Christian Couples Face

Even Abstaining from Premarital Sex Can Cause Problems

by Grace H. Ketterman

ON THEIR SIX-WEEK ANNIVERSARY, the groom bought six red roses. After work, he hurried to beat his lovely bride home. There, he carefully placed each flower in a place he knew she traveled every evening.

He put one by her water glass, one in the refrigerator, one where she changed clothes. By the time she would be ready to relax, she would have collected the entire bouquet.

This young man was a romantic groom. And he tried hard to be a good husband and a good lover.

But after six months of trying, he began to fear his wife would never learn to enjoy sex. He finally asked her what he was doing wrong and how they could make their physical intimacy fun for both.

Her reply was, "I don't need sex, and I'm not very good at it."

The unstated implication was this: "Furthermore, I don't care at all about your needs or feelings."

This story is true. And it is only one of many stories about sexual problems Christian couples face.

I'm happy to tell you that one thing I've learned from my years of counseling married couples is that all the common sexual-related problems Christians face can be solved if both spouses will work at finding the answers.

Five Common Problems

1. Sexual abstinence before marriage can create such strong inhibitions it is difficult to suddenly relax those restraints after the wedding.

This problem has become a rare one today. Society no longer frowns on couples who engage in sexual intimacy before marriage. Television and the printed media portray premarital sex as natural. Christians, too, are practicing the new morality that the world is preaching.

Sex before marriage is not normal, and it is not Christian. The commitment of engagement can allow for a healthy, gradual increase in affection, preparing couples for a joyful wedding night. But setting and staying within the boundaries during the engagement demands strong self-control, mutual agreement, and profound commitment to Christian principles.

2. Sexual promiscuity before marriage can create guilt that can develop into a barrier between the couple.

For example, the basic physical pleasure of an early sexual partner may be far greater than with the spouse. No matter how compatible a husband and wife may be in other areas, it is extremely easy to fall into a habit of re-membering and fantasying about that other person.

Perhaps that is one reason the Bible warns against for-nication.

If this is your problem, you need to understand and practice:

A. The concept of confession to God, receiving for-giveness, and relinquishing that old guilt.

B. The discipline of putting your past behind you and focusing on the lovable qualities of your spouse.

3. Mistaken teaching and beliefs about sex can cause problems.

A woman I'll call Diane sought a doctor's help for what she believed was frigidity. When the doctor finally asked her to describe just what she experienced during sexual in-tercourse, she described a perfectly normal orgasm.

The doctor asked her what she believed an orgasm should be like. And Diane described a thoroughly exagger-ated, first-person account told to her by a friend. This friend had given Diane a totally false impression of what the experience was like. Whether the friend was bragging, talking tongue-in-cheek, or just pulling Diane's leg, the words created false expectations that spoiled Diane's early adjustment in her marriage.

I've seen examples from the other extreme too. These are young people who come to marriage after years of hearing that sex is dirty and bad, to be tolerated as a duty at best. Such mistaken teaching has often spanned a life-time. And it has usually been communicated with few words and many cold actions.

I can only imagine such a family, because my parents were most appropriately affectionate.

One of my most moving memories is of sitting peacefully in my little rocking chair on a Sunday morning. As I waited for my family to gather so that we could drive to church, my parents came out of their bedroom together. Not knowing I was watching, my father gently embraced my mother. Ever so tenderly, he kissed her on the neck, and then they were ready for a busy Sunday.

I am grateful to say that my own daughter has similar memories. She told me she always felt safe when she knew her father and I were in love.

Fortunately, mistaken teaching about sex can be corrected, and married couples can be freed from misconceptions spanning both extremes on the spectrum.

4. Power struggles and hurt feelings create resentment, which is fatal to sexual intimacy.

Many a spouse has deliberately refrained from lovemaking to get even for some hurt the other inflicted. Getting even makes us feel powerful. But it is a childish act, and it starts a vicious cycle that can end in a broken marriage.

Almost without exception, verbal abuse during unhealthy arguments can neutralize all desire for making love. God designed sexual intercourse to be the apex of genuine loving. When someone is overwhelmed with hurt feelings, misunderstandings, and unresolved conflicts, sex is usually the last thing they want to share with the person who hurt them. Sadly enough, the victor may feel so good he or she wants sex to celebrate winning. The loser, on the other hand, usually feels quite the opposite.

A wonderful practice for marriage partners is to make a vow never to retire at night with any unresolved conflicts between them (see Ephesians 4:26). Whatever it takes, swallow your pride, and open your minds and hearts to really hear and care about your spouse. Talk out the disagreements kindly and reach a settlement.

5. A lack of basic knowledge of lovemaking techniques can allow sex to become boring and even a turn-off.

Sex becomes boring when you fail to explore how to give and receive pleasure during lovemaking. And it can even become repulsive when one spouse performs acts that he or she thinks pleases the other when, in fact, the other spouse doesn't enjoy it at all. And the displeasure grows when the two don't talk to each other about what they enjoy and don't enjoy during lovemaking.

Television and popular magazines glamorize sex unduly. They can lead people to believe that with a few mere touches in the right places, a woman can be on her way to a thrilling orgasm. This just isn't so. Touches and caresses that give pleasure to one person might not give pleasure to another. And even when we know where and how to touch our spouse, he or she might not be in the right mood or have the energy to enjoy the experience.

Sexual intimacy can and should be an act of joy, of carefully giving pleasure and clearly identifying what feels pleasurable so that each can fulfill the other.

One of the false concepts about sex is that it is the ultimate intimacy. I'd like you to consider just how deceptive this theory is. True intimacy is founded on trust, giving, joy, and unconditional love. And it requires a person to have enough self-esteem to receive love.

Sex, on the other hand, may be exploitive. And it can involve power struggles in which everyone loses. Sexual intercourse, apart from genuine trust and unconditional love, is disappointing and unfulfilling. Couples who experience this kind of sexual relationship often go to great extremes —sometimes bizarre extremes, such as spouse swapping. They do this to find enjoyment. But in going to greater and greater extremes, all they find is less and less gratification.

So be certain your perceptions are correct—that love, honesty, and trust are intact. Then sexual intimacy becomes truly meaningful, the crown of your marriage.

The reverse, trying to hold together a shaky relationship through even the most exciting sex act, simply won't work.

For Less Stress in Marriage

Here are some ways to reduce sex-related stress in your marriage.

1. Make sure your commitment to each other is solid and your love is honest.

2. Discover how to make love with joy and freedom, creatively and spontaneously.

3. Free yourself from inhibitions that make you afraid to tell and ask each other what feels good and is stimulating in the process of lovemaking.

4. Keep yourself as appealing and attractive to each other as possible. Staying physically fit and sweet smelling are as important as sweet actions and considerate living.

5. Don't base your expectations on the media's glamorization of sex. No normal human can measure up to those physiques and techniques—forget them.

6. Be positive, appreciative, and considerate in the ways you treat your spouse in every area of life.

7. Be aware that God's blessing is the very best ingredient of good sex. He gave us this joyful and sacred act for our pleasure as well as for procreation.

8. Read wholesome Christian books and periodicals that will help overcome unhealthy attitudes and misinformation about sex.

9. Be aware that some stubborn physical and emotional problems may interfere with sexual enjoyment. Seek

counsel from both a physician and a qualified counselor. God made us for himself and for each other's pleasure, love, and joy.

When we recognize this, lovemaking becomes the crown of intimacy—a living symbol of the oneness of Jesus Christ and His Church.

BACKGROUND SCRIPTURE: I Corinthians 6:18; 7:3-6; Ephesians 5:25-33

Grace Ketterman is a practicing physician who specializes in family psychiatry and pediatrics. Author of 12 books, including *Before and After the Wedding Night* (Revell), she is also the medical director of a children's and adolescent's psychiatric treatment facility, Crittenton Center, in Kansas City.

10

Taking Care of Elderly Parents

Are You Being Controlled
by What Others Expect of You?

by Barbara Deane

I WAS A CAREGIVER for my parents for years before the word *caregiver* was even in my vocabulary. But several years ago I learned that I was part of "the sandwich generation"—middle-aged people, mostly women, who take care of both old and young. We are the generation in the middle.

Families have been taking care of their elderly throughout the ages. What is new is the large number of elderly people who need care. The fastest-growing segment of our population is the group over 85. As their numbers continue to grow, the number of caregivers grows with them.

An estimated 7 million Americans now care for an elderly parent in the home. But *caregiver* is a broad term that includes much more than home care. Long before my widowed mother came to live with me, I helped her and my father to live independently. And even if a parent has to be placed in a board-and-care home or nursing home, care by the family continues. If the people giving this type of non-live-in care were included in the figures, the number of caregivers would be much greater.

So, if you have joined the ranks of caregivers, the first thing you must realize is that you are not alone. This is important. You may feel isolated with your new responsibilities. You may even be in shock.

It's a shock to discover your parents are no longer strong enough to take care of all their own needs. It also comes as a shock when you find that care giving is much more difficult than you'd realized.

Statisticians tell us that a typical caregiver is a woman in her 50s. But caregivers are actually very diverse. You may be in your late 30s or early 40s, the last-born child of an older mother. You may be an "empty nester," or you may have children at home. You may never have married, or be divorced or widowed. Either you or your spouse may be retired. You may be as old as 75, taking care of parents in their 90s. You may be male. You may be a grandson or granddaughter. You may be rich or in-between.

You may have volunteered for care giving or been selected, either willingly or unwillingly, by your parent or siblings. You may have "fallen into" the job only because you're the child living closest to your parents.

No matter who you are or how you got there, the one thing caregivers seem to have in common is stress. Often, this is because they're exhausted. At various times, they're called upon to

- Take their parent shopping or do the shopping, buying food, clothing, medicine, and other necessities.
- Chauffeur parent to the doctor and appointments.
- Supervise or actually take over the parent's finances. Pay bills, balance checkbooks, and act as trustee if large sums of money are concerned. Plan for the wisest use of available financial resources for future care.

- Deal with the various bureaucracies that aid the elderly—such as, Social Security, Medicare, and private health insurance. Know what the parent is eligible to receive, fill out forms, submit claims, and monitor payments.
- Hire and supervise housekeeping, health care, and other help that comes into the home (or do it themselves).
- Supervise or personally take care of the parent's physical needs, such as meals (including special diets), exercise, sleep, bathing, toileting, hair washing, toenail cutting, etc.
- Supervise the parent's medical care. Deal with doctors, nurses, and home health aides, and supervise medications. Adapt a home to the needs of someone with the chronic illnesses and sensory deprivations of old age.
- Make provisions for meeting the parent's social needs. Try to arrange visits and outings and find companionship for her (or become the companion themselves).
- Give emotional and spiritual support.

Are you exhausted from simply reading this list? If you are doing all of the above, you are probably not giving yourself nearly enough credit. If you are not doing it, you're probably thinking, I don't know how to do these things. As one Christian Caregiver said at a support group meeting, "Nobody ever trained me for this!"

Exactly. There's a lot to learn, yet somehow caregivers are supposed to be instant experts on the legal and medical aspects of aging and also know how to give intense personal care while at the same time caring for their own families and/or holding down jobs outside the home. No wonder so many of them burn out.

If they try to do this without help, they may be setting themselves up for great emotional damage.

I will make my parents happy, they think. I will make things better. Instead, things get worse. When caregivers fail, as they must, they feel terrible about themselves. Sometimes they become angry with God. "God didn't do what I wanted Him to do. What did I do wrong?" they say.

Do you recognize yourself in this description? You must realize that no matter how hard you work, your parent is not going to get better. There may be some temporary improvements, but eventually everybody dies. Christians, of all people, should not see death as failure. Yet too often they do.

You also must realize that, over time, your parent's needs will increase while the amount of time and energy you have to give them will remain the same. This can lead to deep discouragement. The feeling that whatever you do is never enough is painful. But the pain you feel is not the last word on the subject. God has the last word: "When you pass through deep waters, I will be with you; your troubles will not overwhelm you" (Isaiah 43:2, TEV). Do you believe that, even though you may be feeling overwhelmed? Do you believe God or your feelings?

Who Controls Your Life?

Right now, the most important questions in your life are: "Can I really trust God to do all this? Really trust Him? Trust Him enough to let Him control me during the caregiving experience?"

Many Christians think they are already controlled by God. But they find, when they begin giving care to parents, that they are being controlled by many other forces. Your parents may be controlling you by making you feel guilty if you don't please them. Immature and inappropriate ideas from your early religious training may be controlling you. Society's expectations of what "a good son" or "a good daughter" should do may be controlling you. Non-Christians may be controlling you; you may be performing for their benefit in order to be "a good witness."

You may think your parent or siblings who won't help are the problem, but your real problem is almost always yourself. Can you trust God enough to give up these other sources of control and be controlled by Him alone? You may receive a great deal of approval from these other sources of control. Letting God have control may be a tremendous struggle. But it's worth the effort, because if you are controlled by anybody or anything other than God, you will be miserable. He may even now be using your distress to draw you to Him.

But to get out from under these controlling forces that are not of God, you have to recognize them. The following examples may help you to analyze your own reactions. Who or what is controlling you right now?

Control by the Culture

In the early states of care giving, both parent and adult child tend to deny what's really going on. In our culture, aging is bad, dependence is taboo, and any sign that this may be happening arouses great anxiety. The care of elderly relatives forces you to face things you'd rather not face and think about things you'd rather not think about, such as your own death. Denial is nature's way of protecting you from whatever you find too threatening.

Fear of aging is deeply ingrained in our culture. We tend to think aging happens to other people, but not to me nor to my loved one. But it does, and outsiders will usually see it before we do.

What can you do if you see what's happening but your

parent refuses to admit it? Perhaps nothing if your parent is really stubborn. Your parent's denial will usually end with a crisis, such as a fall or an illness; then it's no longer possible to keep up the pretense that all is well.

Denial by caregivers can also be caused by fear of their own emotions or of others' disapproval. They think, I could never put my mother in a nursing home. It would make me feel too guilty. This attitude can be dangerous if it puts the elder at risk.

Alma had been warned by her mother's doctor that her mother, who had Alzheimer's disease, was no longer capable of living alone. But Alma couldn't bear to end her mother's independence. So she denied that her mother was really "that bad." The doctor was exaggerating.

One day, an out-of-work youth on drugs followed Alma's mother home from a convenience store. Her mother was no longer capable of realizing that it was not safe to let him in. She opened the door and he beat and robbed her. Alma thought she had been acting out of love for her mother, but she was really being controlled by her own emotions. Our culture doesn't approve of putting parents in nursing homes; if you do, you're going to feel bad about yourself. So Alma felt good about herself—until her mother got hurt. Then she paid a terrible price in guilt for her self-delusion.

Control by False Guilt

Sometimes, what caregivers call "guilt" may actually be sadness about not being able to do what they would like to do for an elderly loved one. They won't be able to "fix" old age no matter how hard they try. This causes deep distress, which is sometimes mistaken for guilt.

A caregiver begins to feel guilty because she can enjoy life while her frail, elderly parent is confined by his disabilities to one room. She may begin to stay home because going out under these circumstances makes her feel guilty. This distress may also be a way of saying, "My parent shouldn't be like this. This shouldn't be happening to him."

But each person ages in his own way and in his own time, and not according to the caregiver's (or anybody else's) blueprint. Now is your parent's time to grow old and die, not yours. Even if you would like to, you can't share this experience.

Trying to share it is not healthy care giving. You are not required to suffer somebody else's pain for him. "Bear one another's burdens, and so fulfil the law of Christ" (Galatians 6:2, RSV) is frequently taken out of context and applied unconditionally. But if you read on, verse 5 says, "For each man will have to bear his own load." Everybody is given his own life to live, and the burdens and sorrows that come with it are his alone. Others can help him, but they can't shoulder his burden along with their own. You can help your parent with the burdens of his old age, but you can't be old for him.

Control by the Parent

When children are young, they want to win their parents' approval, and parents can easily control children by making them feel guilty if they do anything the parents disapprove of. Mature parents no longer try to control adult children, and mature adult children no longer feel guilty when they don't please their parents. But not everybody is mature. Some elderly parents and adult children make it to the care-giving stage with this childish pattern of behavior still intact.

Elizabeth and Joe were brought up to "never talk back to your parents." When Joe's father, a retired pastor, moved in with them at the age of 88, he was still the autocrat of

Joe's childhood. Whenever Papa did or said something to upset Elizabeth, Joe told her, "Don't say anything. He'll never change."

This policy left Elizabeth seething with suppressed rage and created unbearable tension in the household. The result of trying to keep the peace in this way was anything but peaceful, because Joe couldn't set reasonable limits on his father's behavior or defend his wife from attack without feeling guilty.

This was a false guilt. Joe was no longer a little child. He was a married man whose first loyalty should have been to his wife. But in relating to his father, he still felt like a little child inside.

To be controlled by God rather than by his parent, Joe will have to learn to stand up to his father and say no. If you have never said no to a parent, this will be difficult. It does not have to be done disrespectfully. Almost always, the parent who is approached firmly but lovingly learns to adjust to the new relationship. But even if she does not, you will be free to do what God wants you to do. And He wants you to grow up.

Many people are brought up to be "pleasers." When they're able to please others, they feel good about themselves. There may be nothing wrong with this until they become caregivers. Parents want to be independent, but they need to be helped. When their needs are incompatible with their wants, it becomes a no-win situation for the caregiver who hopes to please them.

Dawn's mother was constantly angry at her, and Dawn was becoming furious. She held down a full-time job and visited her mother in a board-and-care home at least once a week. She also took her mother to the doctor, ran all her errands, and did as much as she could to make her mother's life better.

But the more she did, the less her mother liked it. Nothing Dawn did met with her approval. She even complained about her to the aides in the home.

What Dawn's mother needed was exactly the kind of care she was receiving. But what she wanted was something Dawn could not give her: her health and independence. Dawn was trying to please her mother by constantly trying to meet her demands for more services. This would never work because the demands were a poor substitute for what her mother really wanted. Meanwhile, the constantly escalating demands were a way of keeping Dawn under her control.

The only way to break these chains is to stop trying to please your parent. Like the child controlled by guilt, you must learn to say no. This means you must also learn to say no to your own desire to feel good by pleasing others. The key is to look to God and not to your parent for approval. The approval of other caregivers who understand can also help you to give up your need for your parent's approval.

This will not be easy, but it can be done. But Dawn and Joe eventually learned to say no and were freed from their controlling parents. If you recognize yourself in these stories, there's hope for you, too.

Control by Other Christians

Both Christians and non-Christians seem to have well-defined ideas about what a Christian is "supposed" to do. Living up to this image is one of the greatest burdens that can be put on a caregiver. Polishing this image may eventually keep you too busy to pay attention to what God really wants from you.

Sharon had taken care of her mother, who was confined to a wheelchair, for years in her home. Many people from Sharon's church had told her what an inspiration she was to them. She was becoming increasingly exhausted by the demands of care giving, but she never complained.

One day, looking and feeling very stressed-out, she went to a church luncheon, where she happened to sit next to an older visitor from out of town. She began talking to her about taking care of her mother and how tired she was.

"Don't you have any brothers or sisters?" the visitor asked.

"Two brothers, but what could they do?" Sharon replied.

"Have you ever asked them for money so that you could hire help?"

"I couldn't do that!" Sharon gasped.

The visitor looked her in the eye and said, "Honey, that's your pride talking. You know pride's sin, don't you?"

Sharon went home almost in tears. The woman was right! Her brothers were not Christians, and she didn't want to tarnish her Christian image by admitting to them that she couldn't handle everything herself. People in church thought she was "Mrs. Perfect," and she wanted to continue to have their good opinion. But all it amounted to was being controlled by her own pride.

There's a happy ending to this story. Sharon prayed about it, eventually swallowed her pride, and asked for help. Now, her witness is stronger than ever because, in admitting she was hurting, she has become "real." Her image of Christian perfection helped nobody. But sharing her struggles honestly with other Christians has helped many people.

Control by Past Hurts

Many adults have been hurt by their parents when they were children, sometimes when they were too young even to remember what happened. But these hurts con-

tinue to influence their behavior; they're still under the
control of a past they don't even remember. Other adults
have been hurt by parents in ways they remember only too
well—by divorce or desertion, by abuse of various kinds, or
sometimes by more subtle emotional battering. They may
believe they've forgiven their parents, but under the stress
of care giving the old hurt that was only buried and not
healed is reopened and hurts as painfully as ever.

God can heal these hurts. Ironically, one of the ways is
the way of relinquishment. Sometimes, when you have
given up all hope of getting anything from the parent who
has hurt you, God can perform a miracle of healing. That's
what happened to Mary Ellen and her father. This is her
story:

"I was one of 10 children, the youngest of four girls.
My father put food on the table and a roof over our heads,
but he never gave us any affection or attention, and he was
brutal to the boys. My mother died of a heart attack when
she was only 51, the same year I got married.

"We saw my father a couple of times a year. Even
though I'd forgiven him when I became a Christian 15
years ago, I still had a hard time being around him. My
healing was a slow process, helped along by a number of
different people that God had sent into my life. Over the
years, I was able to resolve a lot of problems stemming
from my childhood, such as my inability to trust and my
tendency to withdraw from people.

"My brothers and sisters all suffered too, in different
ways. We haven't had much contact over the years. All we
learned at home was competitiveness.

"That's how it was until a little over a year ago when
my father had a stroke. He recovered, but he was very
weak, and he couldn't take care of himself.

"My brother Mike stepped in and moved Dad to a

lovely apartment in a retirement center near his home. It was a disaster! Dad wouldn't keep himself clean and turned the place into a pigsty. He also got paranoid about Mike and his wife and made up awful stories about them. Mike was so upset. He'd tried so hard and here was Dad, yelling and screaming at him. Finally, he told the rest of the family, 'I've had it!' He had 40 years of anger built up inside him, and he couldn't take it anymore.

"The rest of us panicked. We were afraid he might have to come and live with us. Dad was too disruptive— it'd never work. Most of my brothers and sisters flatly refused to have anything to do with him. I got scared and called my older brother Don, who lives in Washington.

"Don is not a Christian, but he's been in therapy and learned to forgive his father, so he was confident he could handle him. He wrote a terrific letter and sent copies to all the family, inviting them to a family meeting at Mike's home. He outlined the situation and told them we were going to make some decisions about Dad's future. He invited Dad too.

"Don really confronted Dad, right there in front of all of us. About how he wouldn't take baths or change his clothes. I was so embarrassed I didn't know where to look. Dad just ignored him.

"So Don asked us, 'What are you each willing to do?'

"We listed Dad's needs. We decided he couldn't live with any of his children. He'd never cooperated in a home situation before, and it wasn't likely he'd start now. And everybody but Mike lived too far away to come in to help him.

"We came up with a plan: we would hire somebody for eight hours per week to help him with personal care. Dad would pay Mike's wife, who'd been cleaning his apartment, to continue. The three children who were willing would call him weekly to check on him. I would take over handling his finances. I'd come over once a month to write checks and see that his bills were paid.

"Don even figured out that it would cost each of us 67 cents a day to take care of our father! Then he circulated another letter to the family, describing the plan. Only those who wanted to would take part, and each of us would do only what he wanted to do. He wrote a letter to Dad, enclosing a copy of this letter, and asked for his cooperation.

"Well—I've seen the most dramatic change in my father since this happened. The paranoia is totally gone. I believe it was caused by his fear of my brother. Mike is a harsh, demanding, controlling man—a lot like his father. My father had treated him very badly when he was young, and now he was weak and helpless, and Mike was big and strong. If Mike had ever been physical with him, there's nothing my father could have done.

"I think the meeting did it. He had to sit there and listen to what we had to put up with. Dad is an intelligent man, and I think he realized, I'd better cooperate or they'll put me in a nursing home.

"Now my father has become a person I've never known before. He has a sense of humor. I can kid around with him. He expresses gratitude to me. He's even phoned me—which he had never done before in my whole life. I enjoy my visits. I take him out to eat. I ask him all kinds of personal questions and he responds. He even calls me 'Honey.'

"It's still not easy for me to show him affection. I always kiss him hello and good-bye, but I've never hugged him. I think that'd make him uncomfortable. But I do take his arm when we're walking together, and he seems to like that. I never dreamed this would be possible.

"Now I know my healing is complete. I'm no longer

this poor little girl whose father didn't love her, which meant, of course, that she must have been unlovable. I'm praying that my brothers and sisters can come to know the Lord and experience some of this too."

None of this would have happened if Mary Ellen had walked into this care-giving situation with any expectations whatsoever of receiving anything from her father. She'd already given him up, mourned the loss of the loving father she'd never had, and was healed of her deep childhood hurt. Then and only then was she free to act toward her father as God wanted her to. She did not feel any coercion or guilt. She was no longer angry and hurt. She allowed God to act in this situation, and He did—miraculously, beyond all expectations.

But the struggle during the years that preceded this story is what made it possible. In these struggles, God is refining gold for His kingdom.

As a caregiver, you will learn a great deal about the needs of the aging, about what to do about medical and legal problems, about nursing home regulations and Medicare forms.

But the most important lessons are the spiritual ones. There is a great deal to be learned from the elderly. And God will also teach you a great deal about yourself. Even if you don't see the kind of miracle that Mary Ellen has experienced, you will emerge a better and stronger person. Trust God for that.

BACKGROUND SCRIPTURE: Isaiah 43:2; Galatians 6:2; I Timothy 5:4

Barbara Deane is a free-lance writer and cofounder of Christian Caregivers, a support group for people who care for their elderly parents at home. She took care of her widowed mother for eight years. This chapter is reprinted from *Caring for Your Aging Parents*, by Barbara Deane, © 1989, NavPress. Used by permission. All rights reserved.

11

Recovering from Grief
Is like Climbing a Ladder

*A Pastor Begins the Climb
When His Wife and Child Die
in the Delivery Room*

by Dwight "Ike" Reighard

I COULD STILL HEAR THE WORDS "Code 100 to labor and delivery" blasting through the intercom at Piedmont Hospital. I ran toward Cindy's room. Somehow I knew that emergency alarm signaled trouble for my wife.

"She's dead, isn't she?" I asked.

"No, not yet," the doctor responded quietly.

"Please don't lie to me!"

"I'm not," he tried to reassure me. "They've got a heartbeat, but they can't keep her blood pressure up. They're doing everything they can."

Only moments earlier, Cindy had been vibrant as she sent me to tell our family and friends that her pain had eased and that it wouldn't be long until the baby would be here. Less than an hour later, Cindy's obstetrician came out of the room where Cindy lay motionless. I could read his face.

"It's over, isn't it?" I asked.

"Yes, we've been working on her for about 50 minutes. Ike, I'm sorry."

Weeks later, I still could not comprehend the reason for Cindy's death. The doctor explained Cindy had died of an amniotic fluid embolism, a phenomenon about which medical science knows little. Only one mother out of thousands encounters the condition, and rarely is one stricken before reaching the stage of delivery. Why Cindy?

In the months following Cindy's death, my grief took its toll. My robust imagination worked double time to produce a network of emotions. I hotly debated all the "whys" of life and death. I don't believe for a moment that it is unspiritual for a Christian to ask "why?" when experiencing a heartbreak.

Although I have seen positive things come out of the death of Cindy and the baby, I've never really settled in my mind why they died. The why questions that bombarded me at the time of Cindy's funeral persisted as I tried to live without her. Why would He cut her life short? Why would He give us the baby and then take them both?

Cindy's spiritual strength had been so important to me. Why did God take it away? I asked myself if I thought He took Cindy to punish me. I finally concluded that couldn't be the case—God didn't have to go through Cindy or the baby to get to me.

Well, I continued to challenge, maybe God is out of control. Maybe evil has triumphed. That frightening prospect was a real consideration as my sorrow battered me back and forth.

Because I couldn't answer "why?" I turned to asking "why now?" Why, when life seemed perfect, did God take Cindy? But in facing "why now?" I had to consider "When would have been a good time for Cindy to die?" After the baby was born? When the baby was 4 years old? . . . or 10? After 40 years of marriage? . . . or 50?

The next question was "why me?" But to entertain that viewpoint would imply that it was OK for someone else to suffer—as long as it didn't touch me.

I finally realized that I was losing the battle. I didn't want to be a slave to questions that have no answers. C. S. Lewis, in *A Grief Observed*, said as he mourned for his wife:

"When I lay these questions before God I get no answer. But a rather special sort of 'no answer.' It is not the locked door. It is more like a silent, certainly not uncompassionate, gaze. As though He shook His head not in refusal but waiving the question. 'Peace, child; you don't understand.'"

I came to see that the thing to do was to leave my questions with God.

With waning emotional strength, I reached for my most brutal weapon—anger.

Rodney, a good friend of mine, and I took a trip to Florida for a few days of rest. While lounging by the pool one day, I was joined by a woman who wanted to be friendly. "Well, what brings you to Florida?" she asked. Intending to share my misery, I snarled back, "My wife died." The woman's expression confirmed that I'd set her completely adrift. I didn't even care.

Desperately lonely, I had become a stranger to myself. Pain and confusion kept swelling inside me. I wondered how I would contain it and still go on as a decent, caring human being.

One Rung at a Time

Relief from grief never comes overnight. Recovery is like a ladder we climb one rung at a time. I knew I would find my answers in God. I knew somehow He was going to take care of me, but the wounds remained as I searched for the way in which He would bring healing.

People gave me advice from all directions. Christians told me to "Hang in there and pray." I did my best, but eventually I discovered that while hanging and praying made for an impressive spiritual testimony, it was not the total solution. I needed some insight and support from someone trained to counsel.

Ron Braund, director of a counseling service, agreed to meet with me. Our meetings weren't always structured. At times we went to McDonald's. Sometimes Ron came to my office; sometimes I went to his.

Objective and unbiased, Ron let me say anything. I could vent my anger, frustration, and fears. He never judged. Ron asked me questions I didn't know how to ask myself. He touched on feelings I couldn't define.

Throughout this time, following the will of God, being a respectable pastor, and being loyal to Cindy and those who loved her were three principles that were very important to me.

Because I believed some of my feelings—such as wanting to have a happy life and to do some things that were fun—were inappropriate, I attempted to disregard them. I didn't realize these unmet needs were a valid consideration. When I sought to stand by my values, my needs were repressed. When I tried to get my needs met, I created a values conflict.

Failing to "get it right," I moved from self-respect, to self-contempt, to depression, to emotional burnout. Without some clarification, self-destruction could have been the ultimate outcome.

I wondered what those under my leadership would think if they really knew me. I felt I couldn't possibly ask them, but I also wondered how those in a similar turmoil were making it through their dark hours.

With Ron's guidance, I saw that the answer was within me. I had to reach into myself, use my God-given resources to solve the problem. I had to accept my limitations and give up the pretense of being more than I was. I also had to make a conscious choice to face my needs and fill them, trusting God to guide me.

In the spiritual realm, I learned that I could receive the joy of the Lord and get on with my life whenever I chose to do so. As Ron said, "If you make the choice, God will make the change." If I launched out on faith in Him, He would prove trustworthy.

I learned something about God that I'd never needed before. He was pulling for me. He wanted me to move from grief to joy. I determined to accept with gratitude the healing God offered.

Ron and I also reviewed the "why" questions that I had learned to leave unanswered. He taught me to go from "why?" to "what?" What are You doing, God? What can I take away from this experience that will benefit me and others? What in this situation will ultimately bring glory to You?

Growth Begins

As my insights grew, I could see that the ladder of recovery was a ladder of growth. The maturing life was one in which I achieved new and different perspectives. The final and perfect perspective is at the top with God. Certainly I would not overcome all my perplexities in this world, but the closer I got to Him, the higher and better would be my viewing point.

I learned in a new way to appreciate the words of Jesus to Paul, "My grace is sufficient for you, for my power is made perfect in weakness." And with it, I grasped a new sense of Paul's own testimony: "Therefore I will boast all the more gladly about my weaknesses, so that Christ's power may rest on me. That is why, for Christ's sake, I delight in weaknesses, in insults, in hardships, in persecutions, in difficulties. For when I am weak, then I am strong" (2 Corinthians 12:9-10).

I climbed yet another rung in my recovery ladder one day when an acquaintance, Ralph Cooper, came to see me. His wife had died a few years earlier, which put him in a position to say, "I know what you are feeling." Ralph had heard me say of Cindy's death, "I'll never get over it."

"You're right, Ike, you never will get over it," Ralph said. "Your life has been altered, and what you have gone through will always be a part of you." Hearing from a man my age who had found love and happiness again was a gift from God.

Ralph helped me understand it was OK to feel as if I would never get over my loss. My life was changed and I would always bear the effects of my sorrow. That's the way it was supposed to be, but the alteration didn't have to be a negative one.

"The great thing in the world," Oliver Wendell Holmes once said, "is not so much where we stand as in what direction we are moving." With new insights and a new outlook, I was moving in the right direction.

I was climbing that ladder. I hadn't gone as high as I wanted to go, I hadn't gone as high as I would eventually go, but, praise God, I was on my way.

BACKGROUND SCRIPTURE: *Ecclesiastes 3:1-8; 2 Corinthians 1:3-4; 12:9-10*

Dwight "Ike" Reighard is pastor of New Hope Baptist Church, Fayetteville, Ga. This chapter is adapted by permission from *Treasures in the Dark,* © 1990 Thomas Nelson Publishers.

12

In Defense of Pain

Lepers Know the Curse of Life Without Pain

by Philip Yancey

THE WELL-KNOWN German pastor and theologian Helmut Thielicke was once asked what was the greatest problem he had observed in the United States. He replied, "They have an inadequate view of suffering."

Ask any group of college students what they have against Christianity, and they'll likely echo variations on the theme of suffering: "I can't believe in a God who would allow Auschwitz"; "My teenage sister died of leukemia despite all the Christians' prayers"; "One-third of the world went to bed hungry last night—how does that fit in with your Christianity?"

The problem of pain keeps popping up. Like Hercules' battle against the hydra, all our attempts to chop down arguments are met with writhing new examples of suffering. And the Christian's defense usually sounds like an apology (not in the classic theological sense of a well-reasoned defense, but in the red-faced, foot-shuffling, lowered-head sense of embarrassment).

I have never read a poem extolling the virtues of pain, nor seen a statue erected in its honor, nor heard a hymn dedicated to it. Pain is usually defined as "unpleasantness." In a dark, secret moment, many Christians would probably concede that pain was God's mistake. He really should have worked harder and invented a better way of alerting us to the world's dangers. I am convinced that pain gets a bad press. Perhaps we *should* see statues, hymns, and poems to pain. Up close under a microscope, the pain network is seen in an entirely different dimension.

In our embarrassment over the problem of pain, we seem to have forgotten a central fact that has been repeatedly brought to my attention by Dr. Paul Brand, a missionary surgeon who heads the rehabilitation branch of America's only leprosarium. "If I had one gift that I could give to people with leprosy, it would be the gift of pain," Dr. Brand says.

"Thank God for Pain"

The gift of pain. An alien, paradoxical concept. One that might never have occurred to us but, as we shall see, one that flows naturally from the experience of a surgeon who treats leprosy victims.

Seen from this viewpoint, pain, like humanity and nature, is an essentially good creation that has been bent in the Fall. It fits neatly into the cosmic Christian scheme.

After years of working with leprosy patients, Dr. Paul Brand learned to exult in the sensation of cutting a finger, turning an ankle, stepping into a too-hot bath. "Thank God for pain!" he says.

Doctors once believed the disease of leprosy caused the ulcers on hands and feet and face that eventually led to rotting flesh and the gradual loss of limbs. Mainly through Dr. Brand's research, it has been established that in 99 percent of the cases, leprosy only *numbs* the extremities. The decay of flesh occurs solely because the warning system of pain is absent.

How does the decay happen? Visitors to rural villages in Africa and Asia have sometimes observed a horrible sight: the person with leprosy standing by the heavy iron cooking pot watching the potatoes. As they are done, without flinching he thrusts his arm deep into the scalding water and recovers the cooked potatoes. Dr. Brand found that abusive acts such as this were the chief cause of body deterioration. The potato-watching leprosy victim had felt no pain, but his skin blistered, his cells were destroyed and laid open to infection. Leprosy had not destroyed the tissue; it had merely removed the warning sensors that alerted him to danger.

On one occasion, as Dr. Brand was still formulating this radical theory, he tried to open the door of a little storeroom, but a rusty padlock would not yield to his pressure on the key. A leprosy patient, an undersized, malnourished 10-year-old, approached him, smiling.

"Let me try, sahib doctor," he offered and reached for the key. He closed his thumb and forefinger on the key and with a quick jerk of the hand turned it in the lock.

Brand was dumbfounded. How could this weak youngster outexert him? His eyes caught a telltale clue. Was that a drop of blood on the floor?

Upon examining the boy's fingers, Brand discovered the act of turning the key had slashed the finger open to the bone; skin and fat and joint were all exposed. Yet the boy was completely unaware of it! To him, the sensation of cutting a finger to the bone was no different from picking up a stone or turning a coin in his pocket.

The daily routines of life ground away at these patients' hands and feet; but without a warning system to alert them, they succumbed. If an ankle turned, tearing tendon and muscle, they would adjust and walk crookedly. If a rat chewed off a finger in the night, they would not discover it until the next morning. (In fact, Brand required his departing patients to take a cat home with them to prevent this common occurrence.)

His discovery revolutionized medicine's approach to leprosy. And it starkly illustrates why Paul Brand can say with utter sincerity, "Thank God for pain!" By definition, pain is unpleasant, so unpleasant as to *force* us to withdraw our finger from boiling water, lightning-fast. Yet it is that very quality that saves us from destruction. Unless the warning signal demands response, we might not heed it.

Pain: God's Megaphone

Brand's discovery in the physical realm closely parallels the moral argument for pain offered by C. S. Lewis in *The Problem of Pain.* Just as physical pain is an early warning signal to the brain, it is a warning signal to the soul. Pain is a megaphone of God that, sometimes murmuring, sometimes shouting, reminds us that something is wrong. It convinces us the entire human condition is out of whack. We on earth are a rebel fortress, and every sting and every ache reminds us.

We could (some people do) believe that the purpose of life here is to be comfortable. Enjoy yourself, build a nice home, engorge good food, have sex, live the good life. That's all there is. But the presence of suffering complicates that philosophy. It's much harder to believe that the world is here for my hedonistic fulfillment when a third of its people go to bed starving each night. It's much harder to believe that the purpose of life is to feel good when I see people smashed on the freeway. If I try to escape the idea and merely enjoy life, suffering is there, haunting me, reminding me of how hollow life would be if this world were all I'd ever know.

Something is wrong with a life of wars and violence and insults. We need help. He who wants to be satisfied with this world, who wants to think the only reason for living is to enjoy a good life, must do so with cotton in his ears; the megaphone of pain is a loud one.

Pain, God's megaphone, can drive me away from Him. I can hate God for allowing such misery. Or, on the other hand, it can drive me to Him. I can believe Him when He says that this world is not all there is and take the chance that He is making a perfect place for those who follow Him on pain-wracked Earth.

If you once doubt the megaphone value of suffering, visit the intensive-care ward of a hospital. It's unlike any other place in the world. All sorts of people will pace the lobby floors: rich and poor, beautiful and plain, black and white, smart and dull, spiritual and atheistic, white-collar and blue-collar. But the intensive-care ward is the one place in the world where none of those divisions makes a speck of difference, for all those people are united by a single awful thread—their love for a dying relative or friend. You don't see sparks of racial tension there. Economic differences, even religious differences, fade away. Often they'll be consoling one another or crying quietly. All of them are facing the rock-bottom emotions of life, and many of them call for a pastor or priest or rabbi for the first time ever. Only the megaphone of pain is strong enough to bring these people to their knees and make them reconsider life.

The concept of pain as a gift directly contradicts the common evangelical attitude of avoiding pain at all costs. We seem to reserve our shiniest merit badges for those who have been healed, with the frequent side-effect of causing unhealed ones to feel as though God has passed them by. The church needs to confront pain realistically and to affirm that a sick person is not unspiritual. A tornado bearing down on my house will not magically swerve and hop to the houses of pagans.

Nothing in Scripture hints that we Christians should expect life to be easier, more antiseptic, or safer. We need a mature awareness of the contributions of pain, and we need the courage to cling to God, Job-like, despite the world of pain and sometimes because of it. Christianity calls us to complete identification with the world—the *suffering* world—not an insulated scarfree pilgrimage through the world.

Jesus Suffered Too

There are those for whom pain seems to be in revolt. Bodies wracked with cancer so that nerve cells scream in unison a message to the brain that cannot be heeded. Muscular athletes who suffer a freak accident that bruises the spinal cord and condemns them to a life of paralysis and excruciating misery. To these people, all philosophical explanations and all phrases like "the gift of pain" must sound hollow and sadistic. It is as if they are connected to the pain machine in the book *1984;* pain has left its natural cycle and becomes a Frankenstein.

There are two contributions to the problem of pain that hold true in any circumstance, whether healing or death ensues. The first is the simple fact of Jesus' coming. When God entered humanity, He saw and felt for himself what this world is like. Jesus took on the same kind of body you and I have. His nerve fibers were not bionic—they screamed with pain when they were misused. And, above all, Jesus was surely misused. This fact of history can have a large effect on the fear and helpless despair of sufferers.

The scene of Christ's death, with the sharp spikes and the wrenching thud as the Cross was dropped in the ground, has been told so often that we, who shrink from a news story on the death of a racehorse or of baby seals, do not flinch at its retelling. It was a bloody death, an execution quite unlike the quick, sterile ones we know today: gas chambers, electric chairs, hangings, injections. This one stretched on for hours in front of a jeering crowd.

Jesus' death is the cornerstone of the Christian faith, one of the most important facts of His coming. You can't follow Jesus without confronting His death; the Gospels bulge with its details. He laid out a trail of hints and bald predictions about it throughout His ministry, predictions that were only understood after the thing had been done, when to the disciples the dream looked shattered. His life seemed prematurely wasted. His triumphant words from the night before surely must have cruelly haunted His followers as they watched Him groan and twitch on the Cross.

What possible contribution to the problem of pain could come from a religion based on an event like the Crucifixion? Simply this: we are not abandoned. The boy with an amputated foot, grieving Christians in nations that oppress them, survivors of catastrophes—none has to suffer alone. Because God came and took a place beside us, He fully understands.

By taking it on himself, Jesus in a sense dignified pain. Of all the kinds of lives He could have lived, He chose a suffering one. Because of Jesus, I can never say about a person, "He must be suffering because of some sin he committed."

Jesus, who did not sin, also felt pain. And I cannot say, "Suffering and death must mean God has forsaken us; He's left us alone to self-destruct." Because even though Jesus died, His death became the great victory of history, pulling man and God together. God made a supreme good out of that day.

Pain Is Temporary

But Christ did not stay on the Cross. After three days in a dark tomb, He was seen alive again. Alive! Could it be? His disciples couldn't believe it at first. But He came to them, letting them feel His new body. Christ brought us the possibility of an afterlife without pain and suffering. All our hurts are temporary.

How can we imagine eternity? It's so much larger than our short life here that it's difficult even to visualize. You can go to a 10-foot blackboard and draw a line from one side to another. Then, make a one-inch dot in that line. To a microscopic germ cell, sitting in the midst of that one-inch dot, it would look enormous. The cell could spend its lifetime exploring its length and breadth. But you're a human, and by stepping back to view the whole blackboard, you're suddenly struck with the largesse of the 10-foot line compared to the tiny dot the germ calls home.

Eternity compared to this life is that way. In 70 years we can develop a host of ideas about God and how indifferent He appears to be about suffering. But is it reasonable to judge God and His plan for the universe by the swatch of time we spend on earth? No more reasonable than for that germ cell to judge a whole blackboard by the tiny smudge of chalk where he spends his life. Have we missed the perspective of the timelessness of the universe?

Who would complain if God allowed one hour of suffering in an entire lifetime of comfort? Yet we bitterly complain about a lifetime that includes suffering when that lifetime is a mere hour of eternity.

In the Christian scheme of things, this world and the time spent here are not all there is. Earth is a proving ground, a dot in eternity—but a very important dot, for Jesus said our destiny depends on our obedience here. Next time you want to cry out to God in anguished despair, blaming Him for a miserable world, remember: less than one-millionth of the evidence has been presented.

Let me use another analogy to illustrate the effect of this truth. Ironically, the one event that probably causes more emotional suffering than any other—death—is in reality a translation, a time for great joy when Christ's victory will be appropriated to each of us. Describing the effect of His own death, Jesus used the simile of a woman giving birth (John 16:21). She is in travail, full of pain and agony until all is replaced by ecstasy.

Allow yourself to go back in time to an unremembered state—the sterile security of your mother's womb:

Your world is dark, safe, secure. You are bathed in warm liquid, cushioned from shock. You do nothing for yourself; you are fed automatically, and a murmuring heartbeat assures you that someone larger than you fills all your needs. Your life consists of simple waiting. You're not sure what to wait for, but any change seems far away and scary. You meet no sharp objects, no pain, no threatening adventures. A fine existence.

One day you feel a tug. The walls are falling in on you. Those soft cushions are now pulsing and beating against you, crushing you downwards. Your body is bent double, your limbs twisted and wrenched. You're falling, upside down. For the first time in your life you feel pain. You're in a sea of rolling matter. There is more pressure, almost too intense to bear. Your head is squeezed flat, and you are pushed harder, harder into a dark tunnel. Oh, the pain. Noise. More pressure.

You're hurting all over. You hear a groaning sound, and an awful sudden fear rushes in on you. It is happening—your world is collapsing. You're sure it's the end. You see a piercing, blinding light. Cold, rough hands pull at you. A painful slap. A loud cry.

You have just experienced birth.

Death is like that. On this end of the birth canal, it seems fiercesome, portentous, and full of pain. Death is a scary tunnel, and we are being sucked toward it by a powerful force. We're afraid. It's full of pressure, pain, darkness—the unknown. But beyond the darkness and the pain there's a whole new world outside. When we wake up after death in that bright new world, our tears and hurts will be mere memories. And the new world is so much better than this one that we have no categories to understand what it will be like. The best the Bible writers can tell us is that then, instead of the silence of God, we will have the presence of God and see Him face-to-face. At that time we will be given a stone, and upon it will be written a new name, which no one else knows. Our birth into new creatures will be complete (Revelation 2:17).

Do you sometimes think God does not hear? God is not deaf. He is as grieved by the world's trauma as you are. His only Son died here. But He has promised to set things right.

Let history finish. Let the orchestra scratch out its last mournful warm-up note of discord before it bursts into the symphony. As Paul said, "In my opinion whatever we may have to go through now is less than nothing compared with the magnificent future God has planned for us. The whole creation is on tiptoe to see the wonderful sight of the sons of God coming into their own. . . .

"It is plain to anyone with eyes to see that at the present time all created life groans in a sort of universal travail. And it is plain, too, that we who have a foretaste of the Spirit are in a state of painful tension, while we wait for that redemption of our bodies which will mean that at last we have realized our full sonship in him" (Romans 8:18-19, 22-23, Phillips).

As we look back on the speck of eternity that was the history of this planet, we will be impressed not by its importance, but by its smallness. From the viewpoint of the Andromeda galaxy, the holocaustic destruction of our entire solar system would be barely visible, a match flaring faintly in the distance, then imploding in permanent darkness. Yet for this burnt-out match, God sacrificed himself. Pain reminds us of where we are, and creates in us a thirst for where we will someday be.

BACKGROUND SCRIPTURE: Isaiah 53:3-5; Romans 8:18-19, 22-23; Revelation 2:7

Philip Yancey is an author who has written extensively about medical treatment of pain. He coauthored *Fearfully and Wonderfully Made* with surgeon Paul Brand. This chapter is reprinted from *In the World*, copyright 1987, Thomas Nelson Publishers. Used by permission.

13

God, Go Away!

The Words of a Pastor's Wife
When Leukemia Came
and Her Husband Left

by Lonni Collins Pratt

WHAT WAS I DOING in a church again? After all, God and I weren't on speaking terms.

Eight months ago, I curled up on the deck of a friend's ship and told God to go away. It was only weeks since I had received a diagnosis of leukemia and had learned that my husband had filed for divorce.

The divorce wasn't a surprise. My husband had demanded I not receive treatment for my illness; he said people would talk if the pastor's wife went to doctors instead of God. He wanted no challenge to his leadership of the small, independent church he had formed after continual fights with the denominational leadership.

"If you would just trust God and pray!" he yelled at me as his fingers tightened around my throat. I knew there'd be bruises.

"If you'd be an obedient wife, God would heal you," he continued as he slammed me against the bedroom wall. A dull pain shot through my neck to my shoulders. I shoved at him to get him away.

He grabbed my collar with both hands. I shut my eyes and prepared for what came next as he threw me against the wall again.

"God's chastising you, and it would be sinful for anyone to interfere in the chastisement!" he yelled, pulling me off the floor by my hair. I looked up at him, expecting the blows to start, thankful the children were in bed.

Then his hands dropped. He realized I wasn't crying. For 14 years I had buckled to his abuse, always begging him not to hurt me. I feared an escalation of violence—furniture thrown across the room, hot tea in my face, black eyes, or worse.

But as I listened to him saying that God was punishing me, an inner voice started whispering, "He'll let you die. He'll let you die because He hates you."

The next day I sent my children to a relative's home, then I checked into the university hospital at Ann Arbor, Mich. I knew what that action meant. He would file for a divorce because of my disobedience. I was right.

That day I stared at cold Lake Huron a long time. Its chill seemed to have invaded my bones. I felt numb. I listened to a gentle inner voice trying to break through my icy walls, and I whispered, "Go away, God. Just go away. I don't want to talk to You anymore."

I thought it was settled and that God would walk out too.

Not-So-Precious Memories

Now as the pastor began his sermon, I folded my arms and blinked my eyes briskly to shut off the tears. I wasn't there to listen.

Here I am, I thought, 31, divorced, working 55 hours a week as a reporter to support my girls, and I'm dying! I've had it. If leukemia is how You reward me, I don't want anything to do with You. If You loved me, You'd heal me. You wouldn't have let him assault me year after year. You would punish him. If You loved me, You wouldn't have let me marry him.

On and on I went in my mental bludgeoning of God and what He would have done *if* He loved me.

There I was, in the third row of a church muttering that I wasn't going to talk or listen to God.

I tried to find a safe place to settle my gaze. It's important to look like you're paying attention in a church that is known for compassionate, caring people. If you look too distraught, someone will want to pray for you.

I fixed my eyes on a man in the rear of the choir—the one who invited me to church. He smiled at me. I should have never talked to him, I thought. When he had asked me on a date, I should have run in the other direction. But he had shown me kindness, and I needed someone to be kind.

I didn't know he was a Christian. I didn't know he'd want to pray. I didn't know he'd encourage me to go to church or insist that I had to get back to the Body of Christ where others could support and pray for me.

God, I said in unspoken words, You have no right to interfere in my life that way! I told You to go away.

The pastor was halfway through the sermon, and I continued to ignore his words. I thought of the first time I walked into a Bible-teaching church. I was just 16. That day, I turned my life over to Jesus Christ. I gave Him free rein to accomplish good for me, no matter what it takes.

In the years that followed, whenever something awful happened, someone quoted Romans 8:28 to me. "And we know that God causes all things to work together for good to those who love God, to those who are called according to His purpose" (NASB).

I heard that passage from the lips of fellow Christians as I buried my oldest daughter—a victim of infant cancer.

After two healthy children, two more daughters died. One lived three days, the other three hours. Again, that passage.

I heard it in a hospital bed when my body had been given more abusive kicks and blows than it could bear. The memory of my husband's fists slamming into my body was still fresh when a brother in Christ leaned over my bed and whispered that verse at me.

After a while I didn't like Romans 8:28. I couldn't understand how this "working" of good things actually occurs.

In my anger I only saw what was "taken away." I focused on the awful situation. A situation from which I thought I was exempt if I followed the rules and tried to please God.

I didn't pay much attention to how I contributed to my problems.

An immature marriage decision at age 16 placed me in a relationship with an angry, violent man, obsessed with ridding the world and his wife of all unrighteousness.

All the years of keeping that awful secret about the man in the pulpit turned my insides into knotted lumps of fear. The fear entwined me until every trace of God was wiped from the world.

Even though I was back in a church, I told myself it was just to please a man I liked. But I knew better. Something about the pastor's voice beckoned me, to just give God a chance, to listen for just a moment. The tugging at my heart wouldn't stop.

A God Who Pursues

God had come after me. I was running away, and He came looking for me. While doctors shot harsh chemicals into my body, I ran away. While I listened to a judge decree the end of my marriage, I ran from the Presence that tried to comfort. Yet through it all, God didn't let me out of His sight.

God put me in that church on that Sunday to hear the pastor say, "You can't run so far that God won't find you. You belong to Him; He loves you. He wants good for you. But if you don't give Him your hurts, if you don't surrender it all, He can't do anything to make it work out for your good. It'll just continue without a holy influence to work for you."

The words stung and yet were tender, as if the pastor had whispered them directly in my ear. I recognized the gentle voice of God's Spirit stirring in my wounded heart.

Despite the many times I had sent Him away, God was reaching for me once more. He wasn't going to leave me— not ever.

"God wants more than that of you," the pastor said. "He wants control of your life so that He can do good things for you. So that He can conquer all the things that hurt you, that bring you down, that rip your heart out. Give Him your entire person, and He'll go to work for your good."

God understood my ripped-out heart. He cared. He wasn't punishing me. No, I was punishing myself.

I slipped out of the pew when the pastor invited us forward. I walked the long, center aisle to the front of a large, unfamiliar church and knelt at the altar.

The pastor, a big man with flowing robes, bent one knee, lowering himself to look in my eyes. He smiled. He didn't say much; he explained that he was going to pray for me and that no one would embarrass or hurt me. While we prayed, his massive, gentle hands—wet with my tears—held my hands tightly.

For a long time, I had it all wrong. God wasn't doing things to "get" me. He was standing right at my side, waiting for me to let Him do something with a mess caused in part by my own unwise decisions. He wants good for me; He always has.

Nearly five years have passed since that winter day at the church I now call home.

Recently, I married the man in the back row of the choir. Four years ago, God's healing power wiped every trace of leukemia from my body.

More important, when I finally gave God permission, He reached inside and healed the wounds I had inflicted on myself.

I don't become immune to foolish decisions, tragedy, or pain "because I'm a Christian." But I am protected by God's love. Life's various excruciating aches can't defeat me. God is making all things work out for my good.

Someday I'll die. Maybe it'll be disease that finally ends my life. But I'll enter eternity whole and healed and well. Wondrous things happen because God loves us.

BACKGROUND SCRIPTURE: Acts 17:24-27; Romans 8:28; Revelation 3:20

Lonni Collins Pratt is a free-lance writer. She lives in Lapeer, Mich.